THE WORLD'S MOST CRAZY, Wacky, & GOOFY GOOD CLEAN JOKES for KIDS

BOB PHILLIPS

GALAHAD BOOKS
NEW YORK

First Galahad Books edition published in 1999.

Galahad Books
A division of BBS Publishing Corporation
386 Park Avenue South
New York, NY 10016

Galahad Books is a registered trademark of BBS Publishing Corporation.

Published by arrangement with Harvest House Publishers.

Library of Congress Catalog Card Number: 98-75417

ISBN: 1-57866-046-7

Printed in the United States of America.

Age

Friend: Was your uncle's mind vigorous and sane up to the very last?
Heir: I don't know. The will won't be read until tomorrow.

❏

If Methuselah was the oldest man in the Bible (969 years of age), why did he die before his father?
His father was Enoch. Enoch never died; he walked with God—Genesis 5:24.

❏

Q: When do you know you're getting old?
A: When by the time you've lit the last candle on your cake, the first one has burned out.

❏

Clem: What do you call a grandfather clock?
Slim: My mind's a blank.
Clem: An old timer.

❏

Grandpa: When I was your age, I could name all the states and their capitals.
Grandson: Yeah, but there were only thirteen states then.

❏

Christy: What headlines do women always notice?
Lisa: Search me.
Christy: Wrinkles.

❏

Patient: How long will I live?
Doctor: You should live to be 80.
Patient: I am 80.
Doctor: What did I tell you?

❏

Retirement is when you finally have the time to sink your teeth into something fun … but you don't have the teeth.

❐

Clem: What is everyone in the world doing at the same time?
Slim: I pass.
Clem: Getting older.

❐

Old timer: A person who remembers when you didn't start to shop for Christmas until after Thanksgiving.

❐

Q: Where did Julius Caesar go on his thirty-ninth birthday?
A: Into his fortieth year.

❐

Quentin: What three letters turn a girl into a woman?
Obadiah: It's unknown to me.
Quentin: A-G-E.

Aliens

The Englishman sat calmly in his garden and watched a flying saucer land. The creature that emerged had three eyes—one orange, one yellow, one green—and fangs. It walked on its elbows, and its nose lit up like a light bulb. "Take me to your leader!" it commanded. "Nonsense," said the Englishman, stirring his tea. "What you need is a plastic surgeon."

❐

Life on other planets must be intelligent. So far, they have had enough sense not to establish diplomatic relations with Earth.

Alphabet

Filing cabinet: A place where you lose things alphabetically.

❐

Q: There's a secret Christmas message in the following letters. Can you find it?
a, b, c, d, e, f, g, h, i, j, k, m, n, o, p, q, r, s, t, u, v, w, x, y, z.
A: No L (Noel).

❐

Abner: How does the joker file an ax?
Abigail: I have no idea.
Abner: Under the letter A.

❐

Nit: I hear that Margie and Harry had some hot words. Is that true?
Wit: Yes, she threw a bowl of alphabet soup at him.

❐

Edna: What letter is a part of the head?
Eldon: I have no clue.
Edna: I.

❐

What do you call a girl who stands on one foot?
Eileen.

❐

Claud: What goes A B C D E F G H I J K L M N O P Q R S T U V W X Y Z slurp?
Chloe: Who knows?
Claud: The boy eating a bowl of alphabet soup.

❐

Edna: What letter is a vegetable?
Eldon: Search me.
Edna: P.

❐

Q: Where will you find the center of gravity?
A: At the letter V.

❐

Cecil: What was the greatest bet ever made?
Cyrus: I don't know.
Cecil: The alpha-bet.

Amusements

Dogsled: Polar coaster.

❐

Trapeze artist: A guy who gets the hang of things.

❐

Who is Ferris?
He is a big wheel at the amusement park.

❐

Edgar: Did you like the carnival?
Emily: Oh, I don't know.
Edgar: Well, I thought it was fair.

❐

Loony #1: Did you hear about the dog that went to the flea circus?
Loony #2: No. What happened?
Loony #1: He stole the show.

❐

Father: At a family picnic when I was twelve, I ran off with the circus.
Son: Gee, was it fun?
Father: I don't know. The police made me bring it back.

❐

What weighs three tons, has tusks, and loves pepperoni pizza?
An Italian circus elephant.

Anatomy

Edna: What has a head, but can't think?
Eldon: I give up.
Edna: A match.

❐

Rob: Where was Captain Kidd's chest buried?
Rachel: I have no idea.
Rob: With the rest of his body.

❐

Ambrose: What is a navel destroyer?
Agatha: I can't guess.
Ambrose: A hula-hoop with a nail in it.

❐

Laugh: A smile that bursts.

❐

Clem: What has eight legs, two arms, three heads, and wings?
Slim: I don't know.
Clem: A man on horseback with a hawk on his hand.

Animals

Rufus: What animal eats with its tail?
Rachel: Who knows?
Rufus: All animals do. They also sleep with them.

❐

What kind of animals can jump higher than the Statue of Liberty?
Any kind. The Statue of Liberty can't jump.

❐

What animal doesn't play fair?
The cheetah.

Ants

What is smaller than an ant's mouth?
An ant's dinner.

❐

Lola: Which is the dumbest ant?
Lionel: I have no clue.
Lola: Ignorant.

❐

Rob: Which is the bossiest type of ant?
Rachel: I have no clue.
Rob: Tyrant.

❐

Q: How many insects does it take to make a landlord?
A: Ten-ants.

❐

Clem: What ant lives in a house?
Slim: It's unknown to me.
Clem: Occupant.

❐

Rob: Which ant is an army officer?
Rachel: Beats me.
Rob: Sergeant.

❐

Lola: Which is the biggest ant?
Lionel: Beats me.
Lola: Elephant.

Apples

Q: How do you make an apple turnover?
A: Tickle it in the ribs.

❐

What do you call 500 Indians without any apples?
The Indian apple-less 500.

❐

Ambrose: What fruit is always complaining?
Agatha: That's a mystery.
Ambrose: A crab apple.

❐

Q: If an apple a day keeps the doctor away, what does an onion do?
A: Keeps everyone away.

❐

Customer: Those apples you sold me yesterday were awful. They tasted of fish.
Grocer: That's not surprising. They were crab apples.

❐

Q: How can you divide sixteen apples among seventeen hungry people?
A: Make applesauce.

Archaeology

How did Noah know how to build an ark?
He studied archaeology!

❐

Eileen: How is the archaeologist doing?
Olivia: You tell me.
Eileen: Her life's work is in ruins.

Artists

Did you hear about the artist with a poor memory?
He kept drawing a blank.

❐

How does an artist break up with his girlfriend?
He gives her the brush-off.

❐

Ryan: What kind of artist can't you trust?
Mark: I don't know.
Ryan: A sculptor, because he is always chiseling.

Astronauts

Loony #1: Why don't astronauts get hungry in outer space?
Loony #2: I don't know. Why?
Loony #1: Because they just had a big launch!

❒

Why don't they make astronauts out of elephants?
Because space helmets aren't big enough to fit them.

❒

Rex: What did the astronauts say when they found bones on the moon?
Tex: I give up.
Rex: I guess the cow didn't make it.

Astronomy

Q: Why did Mickey Mouse take a trip into space?
A: To find Pluto.

❒

Q: I have a little sister, they call her Peep, Peep;
She wades the water deep, deep, deep;
She climbs the mountains high, high, high;
Poor little creature; she has but one eye.
Who is she?
A: A star.

❒

Scientist: Do you know what will happen when man pollutes outer space?
Man: Yes. The Milky Way will curdle.

❒

What happens when the sun gets tired?
It sets awhile.

❏

Laurel: How many balls of string would it take to reach the moon?
LaVonne: I have no idea.
Laurel: One, if it were long enough.

❏

What did the loony astronomer say when he was asked what he thought about flying saucers?
"No comet."

❏

Teacher: There will be an eclipse of the moon tonight. Perhaps your parents will let you stay up and watch it.
Student: What channel?

❏

Moon: A sky light.

❏

What did the astronomer say?
Things are looking up.

❏

Quentin: What keeps the moon in place?
Obadiah: Search me.
Quentin: Its beams.

❏

Clem: Please give me a ticket to the moon, sir.
Slim: Sorry, the moon is full now.

B

Babies

Christy: What branch of the army do babies join?
Lisa: I don't have the foggiest.
Christy: The infantry.

❐

Show me a toddler caught playing in the mud, and I'll show you grime and punishment.

❐

Art: What do you call a baby who is learning to talk?
Bart: I can't guess.
Art: A little word processor.

❐

Nursery: Bawlroom.

❐

Quadruplets: Four crying out loud.

Bakers

What did the baker say?
I've been making a lot of dough lately.

❐

Paul the apostle was a great preacher and teacher and earned his living as a tentmaker. What other occupation did Paul have?
He was a baker. We know this because he went to Fill-a-pie.

Bananas

Q: Why is a banana peel like a sweater?
A: Because you can slip on both.

❐

Appeal: What a banana comes in.

❐

You tell 'em, banana. You've been skinned.

❐

What can you make by putting two banana peels together?
A pair of slippers.

❐

Loony Linda: Don't you ever peel the banana before eating it?
Loony Larry: No. I already know what's inside.

❐

Christy: What did the banana do when the monkey chased it?
Lisa: You've got me guessing.
Christy: The banana split.

❐

Q: There was an apple, a potato, and a banana on the Empire State Building. The apple and the potato jumped off. Why didn't the banana jump?
A: Because the banana was yellow.

❐

Art: What did the baby banana say to the mother banana?
Bart: You've got me.
Art: I don't peel well.

❐

Rufus: What is yellow and always points north?
Rachel: Beats me.
Rufus: A magnetic banana.

❐

Abner: How does the joker make a banana split?
Abigail: Who knows?
Abner: He cuts it in half.

Barbers

Christy: I'm studying to be a barber.
Quentin: Will it take long?
Christy: No, I'm learning all the shortcuts.

❐

Claud: What does the joker call a man who shaves 20 times a day?
Chloe: I can't guess.
Claud: A barber.

❐

Biff (twice nicked by the barber's razor): Hey barber, gimme a glass of water.
Barber: What's wrong, sir? Hair in your mouth?
Biff: Naw, I want to see if my neck leaks.

❐

Gustave: What is the difference between a barber and a woman with many children?
Gilberta: Tell me.
Gustave: One has razors to shave, the other has shavers to raise.

Baseball

Arnold: Why did the baseball player go to the store?
Amy: Beats me.
Arnold: For a sales pitch.

❐

Edna: What has eighteen legs and catches flies?
Eldon: I pass.
Edna: A baseball team.

❐

Little Leaguer: Peanut batter.

❐

Gwendolyn: Why was the baseball player asked to come along on the camping trip?
Godfrey: I can't guess.
Gwendolyn: They needed someone to pitch the tent.

❐

Old baseball players never have mental breakdowns. They just go a little batty.

❐

Christy: What drives a baseball batter crazy?
Lisa: I give up.
Christy: A pitcher who throws screwballs.

❐

Did you ever see a home run?

❐

Q: Where are the largest diamonds in New York City kept?
A: In the baseball fields.

❐

Q: Why is a game of baseball like a pancake?
A: Because they both need batters.

❐

What do you call a guy who hits a baseball over the fence? Homer.

❐

Did you ever see a ball park?

❐

Cyrus: What animal is the best baseball player?
Cornelia: You've got me.
Cyrus: The bat.

Bears

What kind of bear likes to bask in the sunshine?
A solar bear.

❐

Edgar: How much did the polar bear weigh?
Emily: Who knows?
Edgar: A ton-dra.

❐

Art: What do you call a bear that cries a lot?
Bart: My mind is a blank.
Art: Winnie the Boo-hoo.

❐

Abner: How do you get fur from a bear?
Abigail: You tell me.
Abner: Run fast in the opposite direction.

❐

Gwendolyn: What is big and white and scores a lot of strikes?
Godfrey: Who knows?
Gwendolyn: A bowler bear.

❐

Ferdinand: What are white and furry and ride horses?
Gertrude: I don't know.
Ferdinand: Polo bears.

Beauty

Raving beauty: The second place winner in a beauty contest.

❐

Why did the loony girl buy new garbage cans?
To enter the Mess America contest.

❐

Loony saying: Women who use gunpowder as night cream end up with a complexion that is shot.

Beds

Did you hear the story about the bed?
It was just made up.

❏

Why was Job always cold in bed?
Because he had such miserable comforters.

❏

Four-year-old Loony Lucy was visiting her grandparents. When she was put to bed, she sobbed and said she was afraid of the dark and wanted to go home.
"But you don't sleep with the lights on at home, do you, darling?" asked her grandmother.
"No," replied Loony Lucy, "but there it's my own dark."

❏

What time is it when an elephant climbs into your bed?
Time to get a new bed.

❏

Boycott: A bed for a small male child.

❏

What is the last thing you take off before going to bed?
Your feet from the floor.

❏

When is it right for you to lie?
When you are in bed.

❏

Why do we all go to bed?
Because the bed will not come to us.

❏

Leonard: What has four legs and only one foot?
Leona: I'm blank.
Leonard: A bed.

Bees

Arnold: Why did the bee go to the doctor?
Amy: I have no idea.
Arnold: It had hives.

Wilma: What creature is smarter than a talking parrot?
Wesley: That's a mystery.
Wilma: A spelling bee.

Pam: How do bees get to school?
Melba: I give up.
Pam: They wait at the buzz stop.

Nit: What do you call a bee that talks in very low tones?
Wit: You've got me.
Nit: A mumble-bee.

Lydia: What game do you play with bees?
Larry: I can't guess.
Lydia: Hive and seek.

What is a bee's favorite musical?
Stinging in the Rain.

Gustave: What is worse than being with a fool?
Gilberta: My mind is a blank.
Gustave: Fooling with a bee.

Gustave: What kind of bee drops its honey?
Gilberta: That's a mystery.
Gustave: A spilling bee.

❒

Quentin: What is the difference between a bee and a donkey?
Obadiah: My mind's a blank.
Quentin: One gets all the honey, and the other gets all the whacks (wax).

❒

Rudolph: What do bees do with their honey?
Thelma: I don't have the foggiest.
Rudolph: They cell it.

❒

Wilber: What did the rose say to the bee?
Wanda: My mind's a blank.
Wilber: Buzz off!

Bible Stories

Who was the first man in the Bible to know the meaning of rib roast?
Adam.

❒

What has God never seen, Abraham Lincoln seldom saw, and today's man sees every day?
His equal—Isaiah 40:25.

❒

What simple affliction brought about the death of Samson?
Fallen arches.

❒

Where in the Bible does it suggest that men should wash dishes?
In 2 Kings 21:13—"And I will wipe Jerusalem as a man wipeth a dish; wiping it, and turning it upside down."

❒

What did Adam and Eve do when they were expelled from the Garden of Eden?
They raised Cain.

⌐

Why are there so few men with whiskers in heaven?
Because most men get in by a close shave.

⌐

Where did Noah strike the first nail in the ark?
On the head.

⌐

Who was the straightest man in the Bible?
Joseph. Pharaoh made a ruler of him.

⌐

Who introduced the first walking stick?
Eve ... when she presented Adam with a little Cain.

⌐

Why was Moses the most wicked man in the Bible?
Because he broke the Ten Commandments all at once.

⌐

What prophet in the Bible was a space traveler?
Elijah. He went up in a fiery chariot—2 Kings 2:11.

⌐

When the ark landed on Mount Ararat, was Noah the first one out?
No, he came forth out of the ark.

⌐

What did Noah say while he was loading all the animals on the ark?
Now I herd everything.

⌐

What was the first theatrical event in the Bible?
Eve's appearance for Adam's benefit.

Bicycles

First goofy man: I just got a bicycle for my girlfriend.
Second goofy man: How did you get such a good trade?

❐

Why couldn't the loony boy see his bicycle after he parked it behind a tree?
Because the bark was bigger than his bike.

❐

Q: Why doesn't a bicycle go as fast as a car?
A: It's two tired.

❐

Gideon: What do you get if you tie two bicycles together?
Gloria: I don't have the foggiest.
Gideon: Siamese Schwinns.

Biology

Clem: What is a bacteria?
Slim: I don't have the foggiest.
Clem: The rear entrance of a cafeteria.

Birds

Willard: What kinds of birds are kept in captivity more than any others?
Wallace: Who knows?
Willard: Jailbirds.

❐

Arnold: Why did the bird always like to sit down?
Amy: Who knows?
Arnold: He was a stool pigeon.

❐

Ichabod: Where do giant condors come from?
Eutychus: I have no idea.
Ichabod: Eggs.

❐

Cyrus: What did the pelican say when he caught a large fish?
Cornelia: Beats me.
Cyrus: This sure fills the bill.

❐

Fred: What does a pheasant say when it kisses its children good night?
Ted: I can't guess.
Fred: Pheasant dreams.

❐

Ryan: What do you call a little bird at the stereo shop?
Reginald: You've got me.
Ryan: A tweeter.

❐

Cyrus: What kind of hawk has no wings?
Cornelia: I don't know.
Cyrus: A tomahawk.

❐

What do you get when you cross an owl with an oyster?
An animal that drops pearls of wisdom.

❐

Lynette: What kind of bird do you find in your throat?
LeRoy: Search me.
Lynette: A swallow.

❐

Laurel: Where does a bird go when it's ill?
LaVonne: Search me.
Laurel: It goes for tweetment.

❐

Why do birds fly south for the winter?
Because it's too far to walk.

❏

What do you get when a bird flies into a fan?
Shredded tweet.

❏

Grover: What kind of bird eats the same worm eight times?
Gretchen: You've got me.
Grover: A swallow with the hiccups.

❏

Grover: What has wings, is out of its mind, and sits in trees?
Gretchen: I'm in the dark.
Grover: A raven lunatic.

❏

Gwendolyn: What did Mr. Bird call his son?
Godfrey: I'm in the dark.
Gwendolyn: A chirp off the old block.

❏

How can you tell where a rich flamingo lives?
By the wrought-iron loonies on the front lawn.

❏

Prisoner: A bird in a guilty cage.

❏

Q: Which bird is the lowest-spirited?
A: Bluebird.

Boats

Q: Do big ships like the Titanic sink very often?
A: No, only once.

❏

Quentin: What kind of boat is like a knife?
Obadiah: How should I know?
Quentin: A cutter.

❑

Why were the boats all docked in a straight line?
Because they were rowboats.

❑

How do you mail a boat?
You ship it.

❑

Grover: What is the world's slowest ship?
Gretchen: Tell me.
Grover: A snailboat.

❑

What kind of lights did Noah have on his ark?
Floodlights.

❑

Georgina: Did you hear about the terrible accident? A pink cruise ship collided with a purple cruise ship.
George: What happened?
Georgina: All the passengers were marooned!

❑

Q: When does a boat show affection?
A: When it hugs the shore.

❑

Luther: What is the definition of a Chinese harbor?
Lydia: That's a mystery.
Luther: A junkyard.

❑

Q: When is a store like a boat?
A: When it has sales.

❑

Q: Where does a sick ship go?
A: To the doc's (docks).

❏

Ambrose: What is the difference between an auction and seasickness?
Stella: I'm in the dark.
Ambrose: One is a sale of effects, and the other is the effect of a sail.

❏

Q: Why couldn't anyone play cards on the ark?
A: Because Noah sat on the deck.

Books

Cornelius: What book contains more stirring pages than any other?
Henrietta: I can't guess.
Cornelius: A cookbook.

❏

Did you hear that they had to close down the Loonyville library?
Somebody stole the book.

❏

Q: Why not buy him a couple of bookends?
A: Oh, he won't have time to read them.

❏

How can you tell if a student is hungry?
When he devours books.

❏

Teacher: Lacey, how many books did you finish over the summer?
Loony Lacey: None. My brother stole my box of crayons.

❏

Where is the best place to find books about trees?
A branch library.

❏

Boy: I want some good current literature.
Librarian: Here are some books on electric lighting.

Boomerangs

Wilma: What do you say to a boomerang on its birthday?
Wesley: I have no clue.
Wilma: Many happy returns.

❐

Show me a cross between a cannon and a bell, and I'll show you a boomerang.

Bread

Carter: I'm going to put you on bread and water as punishment. How would you like that?
Clara: I would like the whole wheat toasted.

❐

What does a slice of toast wear to bed?
Jam-mies.

❐

Simon: Why did the joker take his bread and butter out in the street?
Frank: Why?
Simon: He wanted to find a traffic jam.
Frank: Did he find it?
Simon: Yes, a truck came along and gave him a big jar.

❐

Kermit: What's black and white and red all over?
Zackery: I'm in the dark.
Kermit: Burnt toast with margarine and ketchup.

❐

Peggy: How do you make a breadstick?
Paul: I have no clue.
Peggy: Use a lot of glue.

❐

Why was the loaf of bread full of holes?
Because it was hole wheat.

Breath

First man (reading statistics from a newspaper): Do you know that every time I breathe, someone dies?
Second man: Have you tried using mouthwash?

❐

Gretchen: An apple a day keeps the doctor away.
Gabe: What keeps the friends away?
Gretchen: Bad breath.

❐

What is it that you can't hold for five minutes yet is as light as a feather?
Your breath.

Brothers

Ryan: What do you call it when your brother has a brainstorm?
Reginald: My mind is blank.
Ryan: Drizzle.

❐

I straightened up my room once and found a younger brother I never knew I had.

❐

Debby: They were planning to add my brother's head to Mount Rushmore.
Denise: What happened?
Debby: They couldn't find rock that was thick enough.

❐

Larry Loony: My brother swallowed a box of firecrackers.
Louis Loony: Is he all right?
Larry Loony: I don't know. We haven't heard the last report.

❐

If your brother had a split personality, who would he be?
Your half brother.

❐

Old judge: It would appear that the defendant is not telling the truth.
Defendant: Why's that, sir?
Old judge: Well, you told the court that you have only one brother, but your sister says that she has two brothers.

❐

Q: When can a giant be small?
A: When he's with his big brother.

C

Cakes

Lisa: What is the favorite kind of cake for policemen?
Lucile: You've got me.
Lisa: Copcakes.

□

Cornelius: What is the gossip's favorite cake?
Henrietta: You've got me.
Cornelius: Spice cake.

□

Lila: What do you have when you were planning to serve strawberries and cake and you forgot to buy the cake?
Lillian: That's a mystery.
Lila: Strawberry shortcake.

□

Luann: What is the best thing to put into cake?
Lowell: My mind is a blank.
Luann: Your teeth.

□

Loony mom: For dessert, you have your choice of good or evil.
Loony Lyle: What do you mean?
Loony mom: Angel food cake or devil's food cake.

□

Willie was invited to a party, where, of course, refreshments were bountifully served.

"Won't you have something more, Willie?" the hostess asked.

"No, thank you," replied Willie, with an expression of great satisfaction. "I'm full."

"Well then," smiled the hostess, "put some fruit and cakes in your pockets to eat on the way home."

"No, thank you," came the rather startling response of Willie. "They're full too."

❐

Greg: Why did the jelly roll?
Peg: Because it saw the apple turnover.

Camels

Rufus: What do you get when you cross a camel with the town dump?
Rachel: Beats me.
Rufus: Humpty-Dumpty.

❐

Q: From what dairy do people in the Sahara Desert get their milk?
A: Dromedary.

❐

Kermit: What animal has two humps and is found at the North Pole?
Zackery: You've got me guessing.
Kermit: A lost camel.

Canaries

Nit: What did the wise old canary say to the parrot?
Wit: I give up.
Nit: Talk is cheap-cheap.

❐

Customer: Are 500-pound canaries intelligent?
Shopkeeper: Of course not! They're birdbrains.

❐

Lady in a pet shop: How much is that canary?
Clerk: Five dollars.
Lady: Good. Send me the bill.
Clerk: Can't do that, lady. You have to take the whole bird!

Candy

Edgar: What is the recipe to make a chocolate drop?
Emily: I have no clue.
Edgar: Let it fall from your hand.

❐

Lisa: What happened to the guy who stole one thousand Three Musketeer candy bars?
Lucile: I can't guess.
Lisa: He ended up behind bars.

❐

Calvin: My brother just opened a candy business.
Cora: Is he doing well?
Calvin: So far he's made a mint.

❐

Q: Why is a stick of candy like a racehorse?
A: Because the faster you lick it, the quicker it goes.

❐

Gertrude: What did the chewing gum say to the shoe?
Gerard: I don't know.
Gertrude: I'm stuck on you.

❐

If you were dying and you had only a dime, what would you buy?
A pack of Lifesavers.

❐

Edna: What kind of beans do not grow in the ground?
Eldon: You tell me.
Edna: Jelly beans.

❐

Nick: Have you heard what they call the new employee?
Rick: No, what do they call him?
Nick: Chocolate bar. He's half nuts.

❐

What do you call a girl who likes to eat sweets?
Candy.

❐

Doreen: Why did the bubble gum cross the road?
Duncan: You've got me.
Doreen: It was stuck to the chicken's foot.

❐

What did the gingerbread man's grandfather use for walking?
A candy cane.

❐

Jeff: What did the jellybean say to the Milky Way bar?
Joel: I have no idea.
Jeff: Smile, you're on candied camera.

❐

What is the difference between a lollipop and a chicken?
One you suck and the other you pluck.

Carpenters

Barnaby: How did the carpenter break all his teeth?
Barbie: Who knows?
Barnaby: From chewing his nails.

❐

Bill: Why do carpenters and plumbers write on sandpaper?
Jill: My mind is blank.
Bill: They like to give rough estimates.

Cars

Ichabod: Where does the joker fill his car's gas tank?
Eutychus: Who knows?
Ichabod: At the villain station.

❐

Bertram: What is the auto-parts store slogan?
Bernard: I have no idea.
Bertram: You deserve a brake today.

❐

Willard: What happens to a person who lies down in front of a car?
Wallace: I have no idea.
Willard: He gets tired.

❐

Nit: What do you say to a guy driving a car with no engine?
Wit: Beats me.
Nit: How's it going?

❐

Where does it talk about Honda cars in the Bible?
In Acts 1:14: "These all continued with one accord."

❐

What city in the Bible was named after something that you find on every modern-day car?
Tyre.

❐

Ryan: What kind of vehicles do hitchhikers like to ride in?
Reginald: You tell me.
Ryan: Pickup trucks.

❐

Ryan: What happens when you stand behind a car?
Reginald: I give up.
Ryan: You get exhausted.

❐

Did you hear about the four goofy people in a pickup truck that went into a canal? The two in the front were saved, but the two in the back were lost because the tailgate was stuck.

❐

What did one tail pipe say to the other tail pipe?
I'm exhausted.

❐

Gertrude: What family car doesn't move?
Gerard: Tell me.
Gertrude: A stationary wagon.

❐

Gustave: What do you do if you smash your toe?
Gilberta: You tell me.
Gustave: You call a toe truck.

❐

Carpet: A cat or dog who enjoys riding in an automobile.

❐

When do Eskimos travel in heavy traffic?
At mush hour.

❐

Gideon: What is the funniest car on the road?
Gloria: It's unknown to me.
Gideon: A Jolkswagen.

❐

Why did the traffic light turn red?
If you had to change in front of all those people, you would turn red, too.

❐

In a car wash: Grime does not pay.

❐

Gus: What kind of shot do you give a sick car?
Gabriel: You've got me.
Gus: A fuel injection.

❐

Christy: What's the difference between the bus and the sidewalk?
Lisa: Beats me.
Christy: The bus fare.

❐

Traffic light: A little green light that changes to red as your car approaches.

❐

Lynette: What is the best thing to do for that run-down feeling?
LeRoy: I have no idea.
Lynette: Get the license number of that car.

❐

"Isn't it disgusting the way some people drive? Just look how close that lunatic ahead of us is driving."

❐

Leonard: What do they call cabs lined up at the Dallas airport?
Leona: It's unknown to me.
Leonard: The yellow rows of taxis.

❐

Q: Why couldn't the electric car go from coast to coast?
A: The extension cord was too short.

❐

A young lady stalled her car at a traffic light one winter day. She stomped on the starter, tried again, and choked her engine. All the while, an impatient citizen behind her honked his horn steadily. Finally, she got out and walked back.

"I'm sorry, but I don't seem to be able to start my car," she told the driver of the other car pleasantly. "If you'll get up there and start it for me, I'll stay here and lean on your horn."

❐

Rudolph: What did the jack say to the car?
Thelma: Who knows?
Rudolph: Can I give you a lift?

❐

Cabbage: The age of a taxi.

❑

Cartoon: A song sung in an automobile.

❑

Christy: Did you hear about the Texas millionaire whose wife was sick?
Quentin: No, what happened?
Christy: He walked into the Cadillac salesroom and said, "My wife has a touch of the flu. Do you have anything in the way of a get-well car?"

❑

Peggy: How many wheels does a car have?
Paul: I can't guess.
Peggy: Six, with the steering wheel and spare tire.

❑

Rob: When is a car like a frog?
Rachel: I don't have the foggiest.
Rob: When it's being toad.

❑

Claud: What does the joker fill his car with?
Chloe: I have no idea.
Claud: Laughing gas.

❑

Where in the Bible does it say that fathers should let their sons use the automobile?
In Proverbs 13:24—"He that spareth his rod hateth his son."

❑

What do you call a guy who likes to change oil in cars?
Derek.

❑

Ryan: What do you give an old lady just passing sixty-five?
Mark: You've got me.
Ryan: A traffic ticket.

❑

What do you call a guy who repairs wheels?
Axel.

What do you call a guy who likes all kinds of cars?
Otto.

What do you call a guy who is accident-prone?
Rex.

What do you call a guy who loads trucks?
Van.

Ambrose: What is the difference between a book of fiction and the rear light of a car?
Stella: I have no clue.
Ambrose: One is a light tale, and the other is a taillight.

Cecil: What was the tow car doing at the auto race?
Cyrus: I pass.
Cecil: Pulling a fast one.

Professor: I say there, you in the automobile. Your tubular air container has lost its rotundity.
Driver: Huh?
Professor: I said the cylindrical apparatus that supports your vehicle is no longer symmetrical.
Driver: Wha...?
Professor: The elastic fabric surrounding the circular frame whose successive revolutions bear you onward in space has not retained its pristine rotundity.
Driver: Which?
Passing boy: Hey, mister, he says you got a flat tire!

Rudolph: What did one windshield wiper say to the other one?
Thelma: It's unknown to me.
Rudolph: Isn't it a shame we meet only when it rains.

Cartoons

What cartoon character lives in Jellystone Park and eats health food?
Yogurt the Bear.

Cats

Ambrose: What happens to a cat when it crosses a desert on Christmas Day?
Stella: Search me.
Ambrose: It gets sandy claws (Santa Claus).

Psychologist: How many ears does a cat have?
Patient: Two.
Psychologist: And how many eyes does a cat have?
Patient: Two.
Psychologist: And how many legs does a cat have?
Patient: Say, Doc, haven't you ever seen a cat?

Lynette: What makes more noise than a cat howling at midnight?
LeRoy: I'm in the dark.
Lynette: Two cats howling at midnight.

What is a cat's favorite side dish at lunch?
Mice-aroni and cheese.

What is the difference between a cat and a match?
The cat lights on its feet, and the match lights on its head.

A catty remark often has more lives than a cat.

❒

Wilma: What do you call a kitten that cheats on a test?
Wesley: My mind is blank.
Wilma: A copycat.

❒

Ichabod: Did you hear about the cat that swallowed the duck?
Eutychus: It's unknown to me.
Ichabod: She became a duck-filled fatty-puss.

❒

Cyrus: What would you get if you crossed a laughing hyena and a cat?
Cornelia: I pass.
Cyrus: A giggle puss.

❒

Rufus: What was the first cat to fly?
Rachel: I pass.
Rufus: Kitty Hawk.

❒

Rufus: What would you get if you crossed a cat and a pair of galoshes?
Rachel: I have no clue.
Rufus: Puss n' Boots.

❒

Gideon: What happened when the cat swallowed a ball of yarn?
Gloria: You tell me.
Gideon: She had mittens.

❒

First boy: My cat ate a whole ball of wool.
Second boy: So what?
First boy: So her kittens were all born wearing sweaters.
Second boy: That's some yarn.
First boy: Well, I'm a knit-wit.

❒

Five-year-old Bobby sat on the front porch holding his cat. A little girl who lived around the corner approached him and said, "What is your cat's name?"

"Ben Hur," replied the little boy.

"How did you happen to call it that?"

"We used to call it Ben—until it had kittens."

❏

Not-very-smart Elliot walked into a pet shop:

Elliot: How much are those kittens in the window?

Clerk: Thirty dollars apiece.

Elliot: How much for a whole one?

❏

Wilber: What does a cat like to eat at breakfast time?

Wanda: I have no clue.

Wilber: Mice crispies.

❏

Q: Where do cats like to go on vacation?

A: The Canary Islands.

❏

Abner: What do cats read?

Agatha: I pass.

Abner: Mews of the World.

❏

Wilber: What do you call a cat that sucks lemons?

Wanda: How should I know?

Wilber: A sourpuss.

Cheese

Debby: Denise, I don't like the cheese with holes in it.

Denise: Okay, just eat the cheese and leave the holes on the side of your plate.

❏

What cheese can't stop talking?
Chatter cheese.

❐

Teacher: I asked you to write an essay on cheese last night for your homework. Where is it?
Student: I tried, but the cheese kept blocking up the tip of my pen.

Chess

At a convention of egotistical chess players in Fresno, the air conditioning failed, and they were told to sit in the hall where more air was circulating.
The manager of the hotel was heard to complain to an employee, "I'm so tired of listening to a bunch of chess nuts boasting in an open foyer!"

Chickens

Father: Isn't it wonderful how little chicks get out of their shell?
Son: What gets me is how they get in.

❐

Gaylord: What is stingy, hates Christmas, and lays eggs?
Gladys: I give up.
Gaylord: Ebenezer Chicken.

❐

They call him King Chicken. He's the biggest cluck in town.

❐

Barnaby: Why did the rooster refuse to fight?
Barbie: I don't know.
Barnaby: He was chicken.

❐

In what place did the cock crow so that all the world could hear him?
On Noah's ark.

❐

Which came first—the chicken or the egg?
The chicken, of course. God doesn't lay any eggs.

❐

Rex: What do you call a hen that cracks jokes?
Tex: I can't guess.
Rex: A comedi-hen.

❐

Laurel: Why would a compliment from a chicken be an insult?
LaVonne: I don't know.
Laurel: Because it's a fowl remark.

❐

Gus: Why did the umpire throw the chicken out of the baseball game?
Gabriel: I have no idea.
Gus: He suspected fowl play.

❐

Little Laura Loony was visiting her grandmother on the farm for the first time. One day she spotted a peacock, a bird she had never seen before. She stared at it silently for a few moments, then ran into the house crying, "Oh, Granny, come look! One of your chickens is blooming!"

❐

Who screams, "The sky is falling! The sky is falling!" and suffers from inflation?
Henny Nickel.

❐

Jeff: How many chickens do I have?
Larry: I don't know.
Jeff: If you can guess how many chickens I have, I'll give you both of them.

❐

Q: What do you get when you cross a clock and a chicken?
A: An alarm cluck.

❐

Q: Where is a chicken before he's hatched?
A: In the Oval Room.

❐

Clem: Is a chicken big enough to eat when it's two weeks old?
Granny: Of course not.
Clem: Well, then how does it manage to live?

❐

Q: Why did the chicken cross the muddy road and not come back?
A: Because he didn't want to be a dirty double-crosser!

❐

Fred: My uncle has the laziest rooster in the world on his farm.
Bill: How can you tell?
Fred: Well, he never crows at sunrise. He just waits until some other rooster does, and then nods his head.

❐

Q: Why did the chicken run away from home?
A: She felt cooped up.

Children

Upscale storeowner: What a sweet child! Here's a treat just for you.
Upscale mother: What do you say to the nice lady?
Upscale tot: Charge it, please!

❐

Teacher: Can you name two responsibilities you have at home?
Student: Get out, and stay out.

❐

Geneva: What kind of toys does a psychiatrist's child play with?
Guthrie: It's unknown to me.
Geneva: Mental blocks.

❐

What would a home be without children?
Quiet.

❐

If you see the handwriting on the wall, there's a child in the family.

❐

Lady: What a cute little boy! What is your name, sweetheart?
Little boy: Connor.
Lady: Can you tell me your full name?
Little boy: Connor Stop That!

❐

First boy: A train just passed.
Second boy: How can you tell?
First boy: I can see its tracks.

❐

Mother: Who gave you that black eye?
Johnny: Nobody gave it to me. I had to fight for it.

❐

The kids were playing cowboys. The front porch became the "Last Chance Saloon." The first boy strolled up to the first step. "I'll have a rye," he said. Second boy followed him, "I'll have a whole wheat."

❐

Little Evie: Don't you like to play with paper dolls anymore?
Little Ernie: No. I cut them out long ago.

❐

We had a kid in our class who spent so much time in the principal's office, they gave him his own key.

❐

Adolescent: A youngster who is old enough to dress himself if he could just remember where he dropped his clothes.

❐

Stern parent: Willie, I'd like to go through one whole day without once scolding or punishing you.

Willie: Well, mother, you have my consent.

❒

Christy: What is a cold war?
Lisa: Who knows?
Christy: A snowball fight.

❒

Q: In a young boy, what is cleanliness next to?
A: Impossible.

❒

Jeff: Go wash your face, Susie. I can see what you had for breakfast this morning.

Susie: I bet you can't.

Jeff: Sure I can. You had eggs.

Susie: Ha, ha. No, I didn't. That was yesterday!

❒

Teacher: If you were dying, where would you go?
Student: To the living room.

❒

An old gentleman, clad in a somewhat youthful suit of light gray flannel, sat on a bench in the park enjoying the spring day.

"What's the matter, Sonny?" he asked a small urchin who lay on the grass and stared at him intently. "Why don't you go and play?"

"Don't want to," the boy replied.

"But it is not natural," the old gentleman insisted, "for a boy to be so quiet. Why don't you want to?"

"Oh, I'm just waitin'," the little fellow answered. "I'm just waitin' till you get up. A man painted that bench about fifteen minutes ago."

Chimneys

Wilma: What do you call fear of tight chimneys?
Wesley: Who knows?
Wilma: Santa Claus-trophobia.

❐

Q: Where does a chimney sweep keep his brushes?
A: In a soot case.

Christmas

Sign on a jewelry shop: "Ring Your Christmas Bell."

❐

I'm not sure it's true, but I heard that in Loonyville they hang spaghetti on Christmas trees instead of tinsel. The only problem is the meatballs don't light up.

❐

Three-year-old Paul came home from Sunday school and asked his mother and father to sing "Silent Night" over and over again.

His parents were puzzled by his fascination with the song, until they listened carefully as the boy sang, "Silent night, holy night. Paul is calm, Paul is bright."

❐

Sunday school teacher: Class, what do you know about Adam's wife, Eve?
Bartholomew: They named Christmas Eve for her.

❐

Sign at a reducing salon: "Twenty-Four Shaping Days Till Christmas."

❐

It is better to give than to receive a Christmas gift because you don't have the bother of exchanging it.

❐

"Your church certainly has an innovative pastor, Miss Prudence."

"Yes, we certainly do! Last Christmas Eve he decorated the front doors of our church to resemble a wrapped holiday gift. His sign read: *Please Open Before Christmas.*"

❐

Art: What do you get if your stockings fall off, your ornaments break, and Santa tracks soot through your living room?

Bart: I give up.

Art: A merry Chris-mess.

❐

Show me a man who's afraid of Christmas, and I'll show you a Noel Coward.

❐

Claud: What song does the mean man sing at Christmastime?

Chloe: I have no clue.

Claud: "Deck the halls with poison ivy, fa la la la la…"

❐

First it's December with Ho! Ho! Ho!

Then it's January with Owe! Owe! Owe!

❐

Some people call running a twenty-six-mile marathon good exercise. Others call it Christmas shopping.

❐

A Carol for the Nineties:

Jingle bells,

Spending swells,

Charge cards all the way.

Oh what fun it is to shop,

Until you have to pay!

❐

Husband: Something just has to be done about the cost of this year's Christmas trees. My neighbor bought one for fifteen dollars and his wife is wearing it as a corsage.

❐

Sign on an animal shelter: "Meowy Christmas and Yappy New Year."

Classic Fiction

Q: Why did the invisible man look in the mirror?
A: To see if he still wasn't there.

Gwendolyn: What does Sherlock Holmes read for fun?
Godfrey: You've got me.
Gwendolyn: The ency-clue-pedia.

Who writes mystery stories and blooms in spring?
Edgar Allan Poe-sy.

Lydia: What do you get when you cross Moby Dick and a Timex wristwatch?
Larry: My mind is blank.
Lydia: A whale watch-er.

Nurse: Doctor, I just wanted to let you know that there is an invisible man in your waiting room.
Loony doctor: Tell him I can't see him now.

Clocks

When the clock strikes 13, what time is it?
Time to get the clock fixed.

You tell 'em clock. You've got the time.

Gerald: I'm giving my girlfriend a striking and timely present for her birthday.

Garth: What did you get her?
Gerald: An alarm clock.

❑

I have hands and a face, but I can't touch or smile. What am I?
A clock.

❑

Bill: Why did the clock have to go to the mental hospital?
Jill: Beats me.
Bill: It was a little cuckoo.

❑

Bertram: What goes tock-tick?
Bernard: You've got me.
Bertram: A backward clock.

❑

Why did the loony man put a diaper on his clock?
Because he heard times were changing.

❑

Did you hear about the eccentric bachelor who passed away and left his nephew 403 clocks? The nephew is now busy winding up the estate.

❑

Timekeeper: A clock-eyed man.

Clothes

Christy: I love to cook breakfast for my friends. Is it proper for me to cook it in my pajamas?
Quentin: It's not improper, but it can be a big mess. I would recommend trying a frying pan.

❑

Laundress (Lawn-dress): A gown worn while sitting on the grass.

❑

What kind of dress do you have, but never wear?
Your address.

❐

Christy: You never seem to age. I wonder if you can tell me how I could avoid getting wrinkles.
Quentin: Beats me.
Christy: Maybe I should stop sleeping in my clothes.

❐

Lois: Why is a wig like a lie?
Lola: Search me.
Lois: Because it's a falsehood.

❐

Gaylord: What is red, white, and blue, and handy if you sneeze?
Gladys: You tell me.
Gaylord: Hanky Doodle Dandy.

❐

Willard: What did the nylons say to the garter belt?
Wallace: You tell me.
Willard: Make it snappy. We've gotta run.

❐

Rex: What did one closet say to the other closet?
Tex: I have no clue.
Rex: Clothes the door.

❐

How do you make antifreeze?
Hide her nightgown.

❐

Geneva: What kind of ties can't you wear?
Guthrie: Search me.
Geneva: Railroad ties.

❐

Why do we dress girl babies in pink and boy babies in blue?
Because they can't dress themselves.

❐

Lois: What kind of clothing lasts the longest?
Lola: I pass.
Lois: Underwear, because it is never worn out.

❐

Derek: What gets around people everywhere?
Dorcus: I'm in the dark.
Derek: Belts.

❐

Lawsuit: Generally a loss-suit.

❐

Handicap: A ready-to-wear hat.

❐

Ferdinand: What has fingers and thumbs but no arms?
Gertrude: I don't know.
Ferdinand: Gloves.

❐

Jane: I had the radio on last night.
June: Really? How did it fit?

Coats

Barnaby: Why are you so mad?
Barbie: I brought my leopard-skin coat to the cleaners.
Barnaby: What's wrong with that?
Barbie: It came back spotless.

❐

Grover: Why did the rich lady buy a Ming vase?
Gretchen: I can't guess.
Grover: To go with her Ming coat.

❐

Ryan: What is the difference between a coat and a baby?
Mark: That's a mystery.
Ryan: One you wear and the other you were.

❐

Patient: Doctor, there's something wrong with my stomach.
Loony doctor: Keep your coat buttoned and nobody will notice.

Coffee

Bertram: What did the coffee say to the police?
Bernard: My mind is blank.
Bertram: I've been mugged.

❐

What did the coffee salesman say?
It's a grind.

❐

Lila: What is another name for coffee?
Lillian: I give up.
Lila: Break fluid.

❐

Lady: How much is a cup of coffee?
Waitress: Ten cents.
Lady: How much is a refill?
Waitress: Free.
Lady: I'll take a refill.

❐

Don West: This coffee is terrible.
Waitress: Young man, I've been making coffee since before you were born.
Don West: Well, I sure wish you hadn't saved it for me.

❐

Q: How does a hot coffee pot feel?
A: Perky.

❐

A man walks into a restaurant and orders a cup of coffee. When it arrives, he pours the coffee into an ashtray and eats the cup and saucer, leaving only the handle on the table. He then calls the waiter over and orders more coffee. As each cup arrives, he pours out the coffee and eats the cup and saucer. Pretty soon, there's nothing but a pile of cup handles in front of him. He turns to the waiter and says, "You think I'm crazy, don't you?"

The waiter replies, "Yes, sir. The handle's the best part!"

Combs

Rob: Where do you buy a comb?
Rachel: I give up.
Rob: At a parts store.

❐

I have teeth, but no mouth. What am I?
A comb.

❐

Christy: What can a stingy man part with best?
Lisa: You've got me.
Christy: A comb.

Comedians

Lydia: What did the comedian say to the cattle rancher?
Larry: I have no clue.
Lydia: Herd any good ones lately?

❐

Half-wit: A person who spends half of his time thinking up wisecracks and goofy definitions.

❐

Geraldine: What did the silly comedian bake on his day off?
Gaspar: You've got me.
Geraldine: Corn bread.

❐

Pam: How did the comedian like his eggs?
Melba: My mind is blank.
Pam: Funny side up.

Comparisons

Quentin: What's the difference between an orphan, a bald head, a monkey's mother, and a king's son?
Obadiah: Beats me.
Quentin: An orphan has nary a parent, a bald head has no hair apparent, a mother ape is a hairy parent, and a prince is an heir apparent.

❐

Q: Why is a coward like a leaky faucet?
A: Because both of them run.

❐

Son: Is a ton of coal very much, Papa?
Papa: That depends, my son, on whether you are shoveling or buying it.

Computers

Abner: How did the joker eat a computer?
Abigail: I give up.
Abner: Byte by byte.

❐

Claud: What does the computer eat for lunch?
Chloe: I don't know.
Claud: Floppy Joes and microchips.

Cookies

Did you hear about the cookie that cried because his mother had been a wafer so long?

❐

When is a Chinese restaurant successful?
When it makes a fortune, cookie.

❐

What is the difference between a chocolate chip cookie and an elephant?
You can't dunk an elephant in your milk.

❐

Did you ever see a ginger snap?

Cowboys

Did you hear about the cowboy who fell in the leaves?
He was accused of rustling.

Cows

Q: When was beef the highest it has ever been?
A: When the cow jumped over the moon.

❐

Rob: Where does a cow go on Saturday night?
Rachel: My mind is blank.
Rob: To the moo-vies.

❐

Claud: What would you get if you crossed a pit bull and a cow?
Chloe: You tell me.
Claud: An animal that's too mean to milk.

❐

Grover: What is another name for a cowboy?
Gretchen: Who knows?
Grover: A bull.

❐

Do you know why the cow jumped over the moon?
The farmer had cold hands.

❐

Ranch visitor: This is the biggest ranch I have ever seen. How many head of cattle have you got over there?
Goofy rancher: Can't tell. They are all facing the wrong way.

❏

Leonard: What has four wheels, two horns, gives milk, and eats grass?
Leona: I don't have the foggiest.
Leonard: A cow on a skateboard.

❏

Q: Why was the cow going to the psychiatrist?
A: She had a fodder complex.

❏

Quentin: What are Arctic cows called?
Obadiah: I'm blank.
Quentin: Eskimoos.

❏

Q: What do you get when you cross a cow and a pogo stick?
A: A milkshake.

❏

Cornelius: What kind of cow goes "Beeeeeep Beeeeeep?
Henrietta: I don't have the foggiest.
Cornelius: A longhorn!

❏

What do you call a guy who smells like a cow?
Barney.

❏

Q: Why shouldn't you cry when a cow slips and falls on the ice?
A: Because it's no use crying over spilled milk.

D

Dancing

Clem: What dance did the Pilgrims do?
Slim: You tell me.
Clem: The Plymouth Rock.

❑

The biggest social event of the season at the Loony Pen Manufacturing Company is the "Pen Point Ball."

❑

What do you call a formal dance for butchers?
A meatball.

❑

Did you ever see a square dance?

❑

Q: Where does a golfer dance?
A: At the golf ball.

❑

Cornelius: What animals are poor dancers?
Henrietta: I have no clue.
Cornelius: Four-legged ones, because they have two left feet.

❑

Q: Where does a snowflake dance?
A: At the snowball.

Dating

Roy: There are at least twenty-five girls at my school who don't want to go out on a date.

Troy: How do you know?
Roy: I asked them.

❒

Rick: Why'd you stop going steady with Lisa?
Nick: She's got her heart set on being a school teacher, you know, and when I didn't show up the other night she asked me to bring a written excuse from my mother.

❒

Jack: I want to know how long girls should be courted.
Mike: The same as short ones.

❒

Rufus: What do teenage boy gorillas do when they see pretty teenage girl gorillas?
Rachel: I have no idea.
Rufus: They go ape.

❒

One year I received 286 Valentines cards. I would have gotten more, but my hand got tired writing out my address.

❒

"If you refuse to go out with me," said the boy with intensity, "I shall die."
She refused.
Eighty-five years later he died.

❒

Marsha: There's no need for me to change the way I look. All the boys like me just the way I am.
Horace: Right—single.

Daughters

Friend: So your daughter now drives a car? How long did it take her to learn?
Broke father: About two-and-a-half cars!

❒

When my little girl got married, I didn't lose a daughter; I gained a goofy son. He moved in with us.

❑

If Fortune had a daughter, what would she be called?
Miss Fortune.

❑

Mischief: The chief's daughter.

Days

Laurel: Which day is stronger, Sunday or Monday?
LaVonne: You tell me.
Laurel: Sunday is stronger, Monday is a weekday.

❑

Certain days in the Bible passed by more quickly than most of the days. Which days where these?
The fast days.

❑

Jeff: What's the cure for Monday-morning blues?
Joel: You tell me.
Jeff: Tuesday.

❑

Q: I am something that every living person has seen, but no one will ever see again. What am I?
A: Yesterday.

Deer

What do you give an elk with indigestion?
Elk-A-Seltzer.

❑

Kermit: What animals do you find in the clouds?
Zackery: I don't know.
Kermit: Reindeer (rain, dear).

Dentists

Dentist: Stop making faces. I haven't even touched you yet!
Jim: I know you haven't, but you're standing on my foot.

❒

Did you hear about the loony dentist who thought he had a lot of pull?

❒

What do you get if you cross a dentist with the Tooth Fairy?
A mouthful of quarters.

❒

Dentist: Let me know if I hurt you.
Patient: I'm going to let everybody know if you hurt me.

❒

Christy: What did the dentist say to the golfer?
Lisa: I pass.
Christy: You have a hole in one.

❒

I know one patient who said to the dentist, "Doctor, I think you've pulled the wrong tooth."
The dentist looked in again and said, "No, I pulled the right tooth. You got the cavity in the wrong one." Then he added, "Look on the bright side. If this tooth ever does go bad, you won't have to have it pulled again."

❒

Rudolph: What did the boy say when the dentist asked him what kind of filling he wanted?
Thelma: I pass.
Rudolph: Chocolate!

Diets

Blessed are those who hunger and thirst, for they are sticking to their diets.

□

Exercise and diet are the best way to fight hazardous waists.

□

Q: How do you go on a Chinese diet?
A: Use one chopstick.

□

Arnold: Why did the cottage go on a diet?
Amy: That's a mystery.
Arnold: It wanted to be a lighthouse.

□

What do they call someone who can stick to a reducing diet?
A good loser.

□

What do diets and promises have in common?
They're always being broken.

Diving

Lois: What do you call a frightened skin diver?
Lola: I have no clue.
Lois: Chicken of the sea.

□

What did the deep-sea diver say?
I'm about to go under.

□

"My business has sunk to a new low," said the loony deep-sea diver.

□

Did you hear about the loony skin diver that failed divers' school? The subjects were just too deep for him.

Doctors

Q: Why must a doctor keep his temper?
A: He can't afford to lose his patients.

❐

Lola: When is an operation funny?
Lionel: I'm in the dark.
Lola: When it leaves the patient in stitches.

❐

Ryan: What is a nerve specialist?
Mark: You tell me.
Ryan: A tic doc.

❐

Ryan: What do surgeons charge their patients?
Reginald: That's a mystery.
Ryan: Cut rates.

❐

Calvin: I had a wrestler friend who didn't feel well so he went to the doctor.
Cora: What did the doctor say?
Calvin: He told him to get a grip on himself.

❐

Patient: Doctor, my child just swallowed a pen. What should I do?
Loony doctor: Use a pencil.

❐

Patient: What would you take for this cold?
Doctor: Make me an offer.

❐

Patient: Am I going to die?
Doctor: That's the last thing you're going to do.

❐

Wife: Thank you so much for making this house call to see my husband.
Doctor: Think nothing of it. There is another man in the neighborhood that is sick, and I thought I could kill two birds with one stone.

❐

Patient: You're charging me ten dollars and all you did was paint my throat.
Doctor: What did you expect for ten dollars—wallpaper?

❐

Patient: What should I do if my temperature goes up another point?
Doctor: Sell!

❐

You tell 'em Doctor. You've go the patience.

❐

The doctor called Griff to let him know the results of his physical exam. "Griff, I've got bad news and worse news. The bad news is that you have 24 hours to live."

"Oh, no," said Griff. "That's bad, but what could possibly be worse than that?"

"I've been trying to get you since yesterday," said the doctor.

❐

A man suffering from terrible headaches goes to his doctor.

"Your brain is diseased," said the doctor.

"What can you do to help me?" asked the man.

"The only possibility is a new brain transplant. But the problem is that brains are not covered by medical insurance."

"Doc, I have some money; what will it cost me?"

"Depends on the donor," said the doctor. "A secretary's brain with cost you about $35,000, and an executive's brain will set you back close to $250,000."

"Wait a second," said the patient. "The difference between $35,000 and $250,000 is vast. How can you justify such an incredible discrepancy?"

"Simple!" said the doctor. "The executive's brain has hardly been used."

❏

Patient: Doctor, what am I really allergic to?
Loony doctor: Paying my bills.

❏

Patient: Doctor, is it a boy?
Loony doctor: Well, the one in the middle is.

❏

Have you heard about the new doctor doll? You just wind it up and it operates on batteries.

❏

The loony doctor opened the window wide. He said to me, "Stick your tongue out the window."
I said, "What for?"
He said, "I'm mad at my neighbors."

❏

Doctor: How long have you had this problem?
Patient: Two days.
Doctor: Why didn't you come see me sooner?
Patient: I did. That's how long I've been in your waiting room.

❏

Patient: Doctor, Doctor, I feel like a bar of soap.
Doctor: That's life, boy.

❏

Patient: This ointment makes my arm smart!
Doctor: Why not rub some on your head?

❏

Reporter (to famous physician): Did you ever make a serious mistake, Doctor?
Physician: I once cured a millionaire in three visits.

❏

Elderly patient: Help me, Doc. I'm ninety years old and I still chase women.

Doctor: If you're that old and you still chase women, you don't need my help.

Elderly patient: But I keep forgetting why I chase them!

❐

Wilber: What happened to the plastic surgeon when he warmed his hands in front of the fire?

Wanda: It's unknown to me.

Wilber: He melted.

Dogs

Ichabod: What is the main ingredient of dog biscuits?

Eutychus: You tell me.

Ichabod: Collie-flour.

❐

Levi: Why are wolves like cards?

Lois: That's a mystery.

Levi: They come in packs.

❐

First jailbreaker: How did you get rid of the bloodhounds that were trailing us?

Second jailbreaker: I just threw a penny in the stream and they followed the cent.

❐

Willard: What kind of bone should you not give to a dog?

Wallace: My mind is blank.

Willard: A trombone.

❐

Edgar: How did your dog get a new apartment?

Emily: You tell me.

Edgar: He signed a leash.

❐

Wilma: What dog is the best flyer?
Wesley: Beats me.
Wilma: An Airedale.

❐

Wilma: What would happen if you fed your dog garlic and onions?
Wesley: You tell me.
Wilma: His bark would be worse than his bite.

❐

Carter: I lost my dog and I feel awful.
Clara: You must be terrier stricken.

❐

Carter: I got my dog a flea collar.
Clara: Did he like it?
Carter: No. It ticked him off.

❐

Art: What did the dog say when someone grabbed his tail?
Bart: Beats me.
Art: That's the end of me!

❐

Ichabod: Did you like the story about the dog that ran two miles just to pick up a stick?
Eutychus: No, I thought it was a little far-fetched!

❐

Levi: Why does a dog wag his tail?
Lois: I have no idea.
Levi: Nobody will wag it for him.

❐

Cyrus: What should you do with a dog that is eating a dictionary?
Cornelia: My mind is a blank.
Cyrus: Take the words right out of his mouth.

❐

Rufus: What kind of dog can fly?
Rachel: I give up.
Rufus: A bird dog.

❐

Rufus: What do you call a meeting among many dogs?
Rachel: I don't have the foggiest.
Rufus: A bow-wow powwow.

❐

Rufus: What do dogs always take on their camping trips?
Rachel: It's unknown to me.
Rufus: Pup tents.

❐

Rufus: What did the dog say when it got its tail caught in the door?
Rachel: Search me.
Rufus: It won't be long now!

❐

Claud: What would you get if you crossed a puppy with a mean boy?
Chloe: Beats me.
Claud: A bully dog.

❐

Claud: What did the joker get when he put his dog in the bathtub?
Chloe: My mind is a blank.
Claud: Ring around the collie.

❐

Willard: What goes tick-tock-woof?
Wallace: I give up.
Willard: A watchdog.

❐

Jon-Mark: My dog has no nose. How does he smell?
Jonas: Who knows?
Jon-Mark: Awful.

❐

Q: Why did the boy get a dachshund?
A: Because his favorite song was, "Get Along Little Doggie."

❐

Why does a dog wag his tail?
Because he wants to.

❐

Gina: My dog has a sweet tooth.
Gab: How do you know that?
Gina: He only chases bakery trucks.

❐

Where do they send homeless dogs?
To an arf-anage.

❐

When is a black dog not a black dog?
When his is a greyhound.

❐

Gwendolyn: What do you get when you cross bubble gum, a hen, and a dog?
Godfrey: You tell me.
Gwendolyn: Snap, cackle, and pup.

❐

Gideon: What dog do you find at the United Nations?
Gloria: I don't know.
Gideon: A diplo-mutt.

❐

Gideon: What university do dogs go to?
Gloria: That's a mystery.
Gideon: Bark-ley.

❐

Buyer: Hey, you told me you had purebred police dogs for sale. This animal is the mangiest, dirtiest, scrawniest mutt I have ever laid my eyes on! How can you get away with calling him a police dog?

Breeder: He works undercover.

□

Gus: What do you get when you cross a dog with a chicken?

Gabriel: I don't know.

Gus: A pooched egg.

□

Lila: What do you say when you call your dog and he doesn't come?

Lillian: You've got me.

Lila: Doggone!

□

Leah: What kind of fish do dogs like to chase?

Lawrence: I pass.

Leah: Catfish.

□

What is a dog's favorite musical?

The Hound of Music.

□

What do you get when you cross a black dog and a white dog?

A greyhound.

□

My loony dog is so bad that last week he was expelled from obedience school.

□

What is the snootiest dog?

A cocky spaniel.

□

Bruce: Have you any meat for my dog?
Butcher: Only a lamb's foot.
Bruce: He'll like that—he's a sheep dog.

❐

Cornelius: What do you get when you cross a dog with an elephant?
Henrietta: Search me.
Cornelius: A very nervous postman.

❐

Joe: Is your dog trained?
Moe: Well, when I tell him not to sit up—he doesn't sit up.

❐

Dick: Why does your dog keep turning around in circles?
Joe: He's a watchdog and he's winding himself up.

❐

Q: How do you get rid of a spotted dog?
A: Use a spot remover.

❐

Q: How do you keep a dog from barking in the back of the car?
A: Put him in the front seat.

❐

Ferdinand: What is a good way to keep a dog off the street?
Gertrude: I can't guess.
Ferdinand: Put him in a barking lot.

❐

Every night the dog brings my dad his pipe, his slippers, and the newspaper. For the next half-hour we all sit around and try to figure out which is which.

❐

Stan: I have a baseball dog.
Stella: Why do you call him a baseball dog?
Stan: Well, he catches flies, chases fowl, and runs for home when he sees the catcher coming.

❐

Our family dog is a good judge of people, too. My sister came home with one date, and the dog took the family car and drove to Pittsburgh.

❐

Q: Why didn't the man put an ad in the paper for his lost dog?
A: Because the dog couldn't read.

Donkeys

Lana: There is a donkey on one side of a deep river, and a bundle of hay on the other side. How can the donkey get the hay? There is no bridge, and he cannot swim. Do you give up?
Lark: Yes, I give up.
Lana: So did the other donkey.

❐

Quentin: What is the most difficult key to turn?
Obadiah: I don't know.
Quentin: A donkey.

❐

Q: Why did the boy stand behind the donkey?
A: He thought he'd get a kick out of it.

Doors

Screen door: What kids get a bang out of.

❐

Rudolph: What asks no questions but requires many answers?
Thelma: My mind's a blank.
Rudolph: A doorbell.

❐

Q: Why did the brilliant scientist disconnect his doorbell?
A: To win the Nobel Prize.

❐

Pam: How come you don't answer the door?
Melba: It never asks any questions.

Ducks

Lana: How intelligent is your loony pet duck?
Lark: That's a mystery.
Lana: Very intelligent! I'll prove it by having him make a few wisequacks.

❐

Lydia: What did the duck say to Jack Frost?
Larry: You've got me.
Lydia: How about a quacker, Jack?

❐

Jeff: What do ducks eat for breakfast?
Joel: Who knows?
Jeff: Quacker Oats.

❐

Lynette: What kind of doctor would a duck make?
LeRoy: I don't know.
Lynette: A quack doctor.

❐

Doreen: Why don't ducks tell jokes while they are flying?
Duncan: That's a mystery.
Doreen: Because they would quack up.

❐

On the ark, Noah probably got milk from the cows. What did he get from the ducks?
Quackers.

❐

What do you get if you light a duck's tail?
A firequacker.

❐

Wilber: What would the duckling say if it saw an orange in its nest?
Wanda: I don't have the foggiest.
Wilber: Look at the orange marmalade (mama laid)!

❐

Luther: What do you call a crate full of ducks?
Lydia: Who knows?
Luther: A box of quackers.

❐

I have two ducks that I use as an alarm clock. They wake me up at the quack of dawn.

❐

What kind of duck robs banks?
A safe quacker.

E

Ears

Carter: I have ringing in my ears. What should I do?
Clara: Maybe you should consider getting an unlisted ear.

❐

Cecil: What do you get if you get vinegar in your ear?
Cyrus: Who knows?
Cecil: You suffer from pickled hearing.

❐

Doctor: I've never seen anything quite like these second-degree burns on both your ears. How did you get them?
Loony Loretta: Well, the phone rang and I picked up the steam iron by mistake.
Doctor: But what about the other ear?
Loony Loretta: They called back.

❐

Gerald: What is flat at the bottom, pointed at the top, and has ears?
Gene: I give up.
Gerald: A mountain.
Gene: Oh yeah? What about the ears?
Gerald: Haven't you ever heard of mountaineers?

Editors

Editor: A literary barber.

❐

An editor at a national magazine calls himself, "The Fiddler on the Proof."

❐

Where should proofreaders work?
In a house of correction.

Eggs

Ryan: What is yellow, soft, and goes round and round?
Mark: I give up.
Ryan: A long-playing omelette.

❏

Q: If an egg came floating down the Mississippi River where would it have come from?
A: A hen.

❏

If in a restaurant you must choose between eating an elephant egg or a 500-pound canary egg, which should you choose?
A 500-pound canary egg, because everyone hates elephant yolks.

❏

Ryan: What does an egg get when it does too much work?
Reginald: Beats me.
Ryan: Eggs-hausted.

❏

Which is correct: The yolk of an egg is white? Or the yolks of eggs are white?
Neither. The yolk of an egg is yellow.

❏

Have you ever seen an egg box?

❏

Diner: Waiter, these eggs are awful.
Waiter: Don't blame me. I only laid the table.

❏

Q: In marble walls as white as milk,
Lined with a skin as soft as silk,
Within a fountain crystal clear,

A golden apple doth appear;
No doors there are to this stronghold,
Yet thieves break in and steal the gold.
What am I?
A: An egg.

❒

Customer: Do you have bacon and eggs on your menu?
Waiter: No, sir, we clean our menus every day.

❒

Melba: I knew a hen that laid a two-pound egg. Can you beat that?
Pam: Yes, with an eggbeater.

Elephants

Q: Why do elephants clip their toenails?
A: So their ballet slippers will fit.

❒

Doreen: Why don't elephants dance?
Duncan: Beats me.
Doreen: Nobody ever asks them.

❒

Doreen: Why did it take so long for the elephant to cross the road?
Duncan: I don't know.
Doreen: Because the chicken had trouble carrying him.

❒

Eileen: How much does it cost for an elephant to get a haircut?
Olivia: I give up.
Eileen: Five dollars for the haircut and five hundred dollars for the chair.

❒

Barnaby: Why didn't the elephant buy a small sports car?
Barbie: I give up.
Barnaby: It had no trunk space.

❒

Levi: Why don't elephants play basketball?
Lois: Who knows?
Levi: They can't buy round sneakers.

❏

Abner: How do you scold an elephant?
Abigail: I don't know.
Abner: Say tusk tusk.

❏

Bill: Why did the elephant paint his toes white?
Jill: I have no clue.
Bill: So he could hide in a bag of marshmallows.

❏

Bill: Why is it so easy to find a lost elephant?
Jill: You've got me.
Bill: It has the odor of peanuts on its breath.

❏

How does an elephant get out of a Volkswagen?
The same way it got in.

❏

What is black, covered with feathers, and weighs 2,000 pounds?
An elephant that has been tarred and feathered.

❏

Gaylord: What is gray on the inside and clear on the outside?
Gladys: Tell me.
Gaylord: An elephant in a Baggie.

❏

How does an elephant get in a tree?
He hides in an acorn and waits for a squirrel to carry him up.

❏

Geneva: What has spots, weighs four tons, and loves peanuts?
Guthrie: I don't know.
Geneva: An elephant with the measles.

❏

Grover: Why do elephants have ivory tusks?
Gretchen: I have no idea.
Grover: Iron tusks would rust.

Grover: What do you get when you trip an elephant carrying a crate of oranges?
Gretchen: I give up.
Grover: Orange juice.

What time is it when an elephant sits on your fence?
Time to buy a new fence.

Geraldine: What do you get when you cross an elephant with a Volkswagen?
Gaspar: Who knows?
Geraldine: A little car with a big trunk.

What is gray and stamps out jungle fires?
Smoky the Elephant.

Luther: What is red, has tusks, and hates to be touched?
Lydia: I have no idea.
Luther: An elephant with a sunburn.

If you saw nine elephants walking down the street with red socks and one elephant walking down the street with green socks, what would this prove?
That nine out of ten elephants wear red socks.

Lana: How many doctors does it take to examine an elephant?
Lark: It's unknown to me.
Lana: It depends on whether or not the elephant has health insurance.

What is beautiful, gray, and wears glass slippers?
Cinderelephant.

Q: Why do elephants step on lily pads?
A: Because they can't walk on water.

Q: How can you tell when there is an elephant in your sandwich?
A: When it is too heavy to lift.

What do you call a hitchhiking elephant?
A two-and-a-half-ton pickup.

Q: Why are elephants gray and wrinkled all over?
A: Because they are difficult to iron.

Q: Why do elephants lie in the sun a lot?
A: Because no one likes a white elephant.

Q: How do you fit six elephants in your car?
A: Three in the back, three in the front.

Q: How do you run over an elephant?
A: Climb up his tail, dash to his head, then slide down the trunk!

Q: What did the elephants say when they saw the French president?
A: Nothing. Elephants can't speak French!

Q: How can you catch an elephant?
A: Hide in the grass and make a noise like a peanut!

Q: How can you tell when there's an elephant in your refrigerator?
A: You can see his footprints in the cheesecake.

Q: Why are elephants' tusks easier to get in Alabama?
A: Because their "Tuscaloosa."

Q: Why does an elephant have a trunk?
A: Because he'd look pretty silly with a glove compartment.

Q: Why do elephants' tusks stick way out?
A: Because their parents won't allow them to get braces!

Q: Why do elephants hide behind trees?
A: To trip the ants.

Q: What did Tarzan say when he saw the elephants coming?
A: Here come the elephants!

Quentin: What is green, has a trunk, and hangs on a tree?
Obadiah: That's a mystery.
Quentin: An unripened elephant.

Clem: What goes, "Clomp, clomp, clomp, swish. Clomp, clomp, clomp, swish?"
Slim: I can't guess.
Clem: An elephant with one wet tennis shoe.

Q: How can you tell when there is an elephant under your bed?
A: When you are nearly touching the ceiling.

Tina: It takes more than six thousand elephants each year to make piano keys.

Nina: Really! It's remarkable what animals can be trained to do.

❐

Q: Why did the elephant paint her head yellow?
A: She wanted to see if blondes had more fun.

❐

Q: What's the difference between an elephant and peanut butter?
A: An elephant won't stick to the roof of your mouth.

❐

Q: How do you get an elephant out of a Jell-O box?
A: Read the directions on the back.

❐

Q: Why did the elephant walk around in polka-dot socks?
A: Someone stole his sneakers.

❐

Q: What do you do if your elephant squeaks?
A: Give it some peanut oil.

❐

Q: How do you know when an elephant is in your bed?
A: He has an E on his pajamas.

Exercise

Willard: Why do eggs go to the gym?
Wallace: Beats me.
Willard: They like Eggsercise.

❐

Where do millionaires work out?
At wealth clubs.

❐

Loony wife: Harry, let's go jogging together.
Loony husband: Why?
Loony wife: My doctor told me I could lose weight by working out with a dumbbell.

Eyes

What do you call a girl who has very attractive eyes?
Iris.

❐

What is pronounced like one letter, written with three letters, and belongs to all animals?
Eye.

❐

Eyes: Double feature.

❐

Q: When is an eye not an eye?
A: When an onion makes it water.

❐

Rufus: What did the dog's right eye say to his left eye?
Rachel: I'm a blank.
Rufus: Just between us, something smells.

❐

Q: How do you know that eating carrots is good for the eyes?
A: Have you ever seen a rabbit wearing eyeglasses?

F

Factories

Did you hear about the deck chair factories that lost money?
They folded.

Claud: What happened when the joker robbed the hamburger factory?
Chloe: I give up.
Claud: Things came grinding to a halt.

Did you hear about the accident at the string bean factory?
Two workers got canned.

Family

Teacher: What, besides a supersonic jet, goes faster than the speed of sound?
Student: My Aunt Gladys when she talks.

Fodder: The man who married mudder.

Carter: I'm on my way to visit my outlaws.
Clara: You mean your in-laws, don't you?
Carter: No—outlaws. They're a bunch of bandits.

If your loony relative was always cold, what would you call her?
Antifreeze.

If your aunt had an upset stomach, what would you call her?
Antacid.

What do you have that Cain, Abel, and Seth never had?
Grandparents.

❏

Rob: Where is the place where part of the family waits until the others are through with the car?
Rachel: I don't know.
Rob: Home.

❏

First man: For the last ten years my mother-in-law has been living with my wife and me in the same apartment.
Second man: So, why don't you tell her to get out?
First man: I can't. It's her apartment.

❏

What sits up with a woman when her husband is out late?
Her imagination.

❏

My husband has a one-track mind . . . and it's the slow lane.

Farmers

A farmer couldn't tell his two horses apart, so he tried cutting the tail off one horse. This was no good because the tail grew right back. Then he cut the mane off the other horse. This didn't work either, because the mane grew back. Finally he measured them and found that the white horse was two inches taller than the black horse.

❏

What did the dairy farmer say?
Cheesy, in a whey.

❏

Why did the goofy farmer put the cow on the scale?
He wanted to see how much the milky weighed.

❏

Gideon: Why did the farmer get a ticket?
Gloria: I can't guess.
Gideon: He exceeded the seed limit.

❒

How does a loony farmer mend his overalls?
With cabbage patches.

❒

Ryan: What is the difference between a farmer and a dressmaker?
Mark: Beats me.
Ryan: A farmer gathers what he sows, and a dressmaker sews what she gathers.

❒

Visitor: You used to have two windmills here. Now I see you have only one.
Farmer: There was only wind enough for one so we took the other one down.

❒

Edgar: How did the farmer count his cows?
Emily: I can't guess.
Edgar: He used a cow-culator.

❒

Ambrose: What did the farmer say when he saw three ducks in his mailbox?
Agatha: I have no clue.
Ambrose: Bills, bills, bills.

❒

Lola: When is the best time for a farmer to retire?
Lionel: I don't have the foggiest.
Lola: About nine o'clock.

❒

Traveler in a balloon (calling down to a farmer): Ahoy there, where am I?

Loony farmer: Ha! You can't fool me, feller. You're right up there in that little basket.

❏

Ambrose: What man can raise things without lifting them?
Stella: I give up.
Ambrose: A farmer.

❏

Slicker: I just bought a farm ten miles long and an inch wide.
Farmer: What are you going to raise?
Slicker: Worms.

❏

Cecil: What is a successful farmer?
Cyrus: You've got me guessing.
Cecil: A man outstanding in his field.

❏

Cornelius: What did the cotton plant say to the farmer?
Henrietta: Who knows?
Cornelius: Stop picking on me.

Fathers

Annie: One time my father shot an elephant in his pajamas.
Frannie: How did the elephant ever get in your father's pajamas?

❏

Arnold: Why did the nutty boy lock his father in the refrigerator?
Amy: You've got me.
Arnold: Because he wanted a cold pop.

❏

Christy: What are fathers from the south called?
Lisa: How should I know?
Christy: Southpaws.

❏

What state is like a father?
Pa.

❐

Two boys were arguing about what their fathers were able to do.
Said Billy, "You know the Atlantic Ocean? Well, my dad dug the hole for it."
"That's nothing," replied Gary. "You know the Dead Sea? Well, my dad's the one who killed it."

❐

Pedestrian: A father who has kids who can drive.

Feelings

Meditation: Inner calm system.

❐

Mudpack: Self-putty.

Feet

Leonard: What did Columbus first stand on when he discovered the New World?
Leona: I'm in the dark.
Leonard: His feet.

❐

Nick: Do you mean to tell me you fell over fifty feet and didn't get a scratch?
Rick: Sure! I was just trying to get to the back of the bus.

❐

Christy: What is the best way to drive a baby buggy?
Lisa: It's unknown to me.
Christy: Tickle his feet.

Fire

Paul: If you had only one match and entered a room in which there was a kerosene lamp, an oil heater, and a wood-burning stove, which would you light first?
Saul: The stove?
Paul: No, you'd light the match first.

Fish

Edna: What kind of fish do you find in a birdcage?
Eldon: You've got me.
Edna: A perch.

❏

Q: Why are fish smart?
A: Because they swim in schools.

❏

Ichabod: Where did the joker wind up for stealing shellfish?
Eutychus: I give up.
Ichabod: Small clams' court.

❏

Rufus: What fish is man's best friend?
Rachel: You tell me.
Rufus: The dogfish.

❏

Diner: Waiter, this fish is bad.
Waiter: You naughty fish, you!

❏

Diner: I don't like this piece of cod. It's not half as good as the one I ate here two weeks ago.
Waiter: Well it should be—it's from the same fish.

❏

Rufus: What fish goes boating?
Rachel: I can't guess.
Rufus: A sailfish.

❐

What kind of fish is the most stupid?
A simple salmon.

❐

Willard: What is both small and large at the same time?
Wallace: You've got me.
Willard: A jumbo shrimp.

❐

Where do fish go to get a degree?
To tuna-versities.

❐

How do you catch an electric eel?
With a lightning rod.

❐

Gertrude: What is a fish's favorite game?
Gerard: My mind is a blank.
Gertrude: Salmon says.

❐

Geneva: What do whales do when they feel sad?
Guthrie: Tell me.
Geneva: Blubber.

❐

Grover: What happens when you ask an oyster a personal question?
Gretchen: It's unknown to me.
Grover: It clams up.

❐

What is the difference between a tuna fish and a piano?
You can't tune a fish.

❐

Luann: How do you communicate with a fish?
Lowell: How should I know?
Luann: Drop it a line.

❒

Why were the sardines out of work?
Because they got canned.

❒

Patient: Doctor, every bone in my body hurts.
Loony doctor: Be glad you're not a herring.

❒

Lynette: What kind of seafood makes a good sandwich?
LeRoy: I can't guess.
Lynette: Jellyfish.

❒

Where should you go if you lose your fish?
The lost-and-flounder department.

❒

Ferdinand: What is a fish of precious metal?
Gertrude: You tell me.
Ferdinand: Goldfish.

❒

Derek: What did the fish say when he was caught on the hook?
Dorcus: I'm blank.
Derek: Gosh! I thought I knew all the angles.

❒

Where do jellyfish get their jelly?
From ocean currents.

❒

Ferdinand: What fish is a household pet?
Gertrude: I give up.
Ferdinand: Catfish.

❒

Ferdinand: What fish is seen at night?
Gertrude: Who knows?
Ferdinand: Starfish.

❐

Ferdinand: What fish warms the earth?
Gertrude: You've got me.
Ferdinand: Sunfish.

❐

Q: On which side does a fish have the most scales?
A: The outside.

❐

Clem: What is in the sea and on your arm?
Slim: Who knows.
Clem: A muscle (mussel).

❐

Q: Why wasn't the girl afraid of the shark?
A: It was a man-eating shark.

❐

Abner: What is the best way to get in touch with a fish?
Agatha: I don't know.
Abner: Drop him a line.

❐

Wilber: What kind of fish has perfect pitch?
Wanda: I can't guess.
Wilber: A piano tuna.

❐

Kermit: What lurks around the bottom of the sea and makes you offers you can't refuse?
Zackery: I pass.
Kermit: The Codfather.

❐

Q: Why do you say that whales talk a lot?
A: Because they are always spouting off.

Fishing

Did you ever see a king fish?

❐

Did you hear about the loony fishhook with a camera on it? It was invented to take pictures of the fish that got away.

❐

Ferdinand: What do you call a man who goes fishing?
Gertrude: Search me.
Ferdinand: Rod.

❐

Q: Why should a fisherman always be wealthy?
A: Because all his business is net profit.

❐

Q: Why do some fishermen use helicopters to get their bait?
A: Because the whirly bird gets the worm.

❐

Q: If you were fishing in a harbor and a hostile warship came into sight, what would be the best thing to do?
A: Pull up your line and sinker (sink her).

Fleas

Lana: How did the father flea get home for Christmas?
Lark: I give up.
Lana: By Greyhound.

❐

Derek: What insect runs away?
Dorcus: I have no idea.
Derek: A flea (flee).

❐

Ryan: What did one flea say to the other flea?
Mark: I can't guess.
Ryan: Shall we walk or shall we take the dog?

Flowers

Derek: What flower is happy?
Dorcus: That's a mystery.
Derek: Gladiola.

❐

Gustave: Why was the 2,000-year-old flower wrapped in strips of cloth?
Gilberta: I have no idea.
Gustave: It was a chrisanthemummy.

❐

What two flowers grow best in a zoo?
Dandelions and tiger lilies.

❐

What is the worst flower to invite to a party?
A daffo-dull.

Flying

Did you ever see a fire fly?

❐

Quentin: What's the highest pleasure you can think of?
Obadiah: I pass.
Quentin: Riding an airplane.

❐

Airplanes: The world's leading cause of white knuckles.

❏

Where does it say in the Bible that we should not fly in airplanes? In Matthew 28:20—"Lo, I am with you always."

❏

Loony passenger: Does this airplane fly faster than sound?
Loony flight attendant: It certainly does.
Loony passenger: Then would you ask the pilot to slow down? My friend and I would like to talk.

❏

Before the plane took off, the flight attendant handed out gum. "This will prevent your ears from popping as we climb."
After the flight, everyone left the plane but one little old man.
"Why are you still here?" the attendant asked.
"You'll have to speak up!" the old man yelled back. "I can't hear very well with this gum in my ears!"

❏

Q: When is an airplane not an airplane?
A: When it's aloft.

Folk Tales

Rudolph: What kind of dress did Cinderella wear to the ball?
Thelma: I have no clue.
Rudolph: She wore a wish-and-wear dress.

❏

Lisa: What's the difference between a knight in shining armor and Rudolph the red-nosed Reindeer?
Lucile: Beats me.
Lisa: One is a dragon slayer, and the other is a sleigh dragger.

❏

Who was born on a mountaintop, killed a bear when he was only three, and swims underwater?
Davy Crocodile.

❐

Q: Why was Cinderella such a poor runner?
A: Because she had a pumpkin for a coach.

❐

Gustave: Who is white, has two eyes made out of coal, and can't move fast?
Gilberta: Beats me.
Gustave: Frosty the Slowman.

❐

Geneva: What does Jack's giant do when he plays football?
Guthrie: My mind is a blank.
Geneva: He fee-fi-fo-fumbles.

❐

Geneva: What man slept in his clothes for 100 years?
Guthrie: That's a mystery.
Geneva: Rip Van Wrinkled.

❐

Gwendolyn: Who carries a basket, visits grandma, and steals jewelry?
Godfrey: Beats me.
Gwendolyn: Little Red Robbin' Hood.

❐

Gwendolyn: What does Sleeping Beauty gargle with?
Godfrey: I don't have the foggiest.
Gwendolyn: Rinse Charming.

❐

First kid: Did you know that Daniel Boone's brothers were all famous doctors?
Second kid: No way.
First kid: Don't tell me you never heard of the Boone Docs?

❐

Who is short, can spin gold from straw, and is very, very wrinkled? Crumplestiltskin.

❐

What is the difference between Peter Pan and someone who quit the bomb squad?

One doesn't want to grow up, and the other doesn't want to be blown up.

Food

Nit: What do bank robbers like to eat with their soup?
Wit: I don't know.
Nit: Safe crackers.

❐

Jon-Mark: This goulash is terrible.
Jonas: That's funny. I put a brand-new pare of goulashes in it.

❐

Ryan: What city are you in when you drop your waffle in the sand?
Reginald: Who knows?
Ryan: Sandy Eggo.

❐

Rex: What would you get if you crossed some pasta with a boa constrictor?
Tex: That's a mystery.
Rex: Spaghetti that winds itself around your fork.

❐

Lydia: What did the nutty guy say when he saw a bowl of Cheerios?
Larry: That's a mystery.
Lydia: Look—doughnut seeds!

❐

Geneva: What kind of soda can't you drink?
Guthrie: I don't have the foggiest.
Geneva: Baking soda.

❐

Geraldine: What vitamin has good vision?
Gaspar: I give up.
Geraldine: Vitamin C.

❏

We had a food fight in the school cafeteria today. The food won.

❏

Luann: What did the mayonnaise say to the refrigerator?
Lowell: That's a mystery.
Luann: Shut the door. I'm dressing.

❏

Diner: Waiter, I'm in a hurry. Will that griddlecake be long?
Loony waiter: No, sir. They'll all be round.

❏

Diner: Waiter, there's a fly in my soup!
Loony waiter: That's funny. There were two of them when I left the kitchen.

❏

Diner: Waiter, isn't this toast burned?
Loony waiter: No, sir. It just fell on the floor.

❏

Where do you find chili beans?
At the North Pole.

❏

Leonard: What do you serve when an oat comes to dinner?
Leona: I have no idea.
Leonard: Oatmeal.

❏

Sign on board at Al's frankfurter stand: "What Foods These Morsels Be."

❏

Q: How do you stop a gelatin race?
A: Shout, "Get set!"

❏

Diner: Waiter, why have you got your thumb on my steak?
Waiter: I don't want it to fall on the floor again, sir.

❏

Diner: Waiter, this food gives me heartburn.
Waiter: Well, what did you expect—sunburn?

❏

Christy: What's the smallest room in the world?
Lisa: I'm blank.
Christy: A mushroom.

❏

Ambrose: What do you call a witch that sits in the sand?
Stella: I can't guess.
Ambrose: A sandwich.

❏

Q: How do you prevent seasickness?
A: Bolt your food down.

❏

What do you call a guy who likes meat, potatoes, and vegetables?
Stu.

❏

What do you call a guy who eats mustard all the time?
Frank.

Football

Geraldine: Who are the most despised football players?
Gaspar: Beats me.
Geraldine: The offensive team.

❏

Did you hear about the football player who was injured one time when the coach gave him the ball and told him to run around his own end?

❐

Len: Gee, I'm depressed.
Glen: But why should you be if your girl said she'd be faithful to the end?
Len: Because I'm the halfback!

❐

Did you hear the loony radio announcer give the latest sports scores?
The Redskins scalped the Cowboys!
The Lions devoured the Saints!
The Vikings butchered the Dolphins!
The Chiefs massacred the Patriots!
The Falcons tore the Cardinals to shreds!
The Broncos trampled the Rams!
The Bears mauled the Buccaneers!
The Giants squashed the Packers!
The Jets shot down the Eagles!
The Bengals chewed up the Colts!

Frogs

Q: Why do frogs have it made?
A: Because they eat what bugs them!

❐

Quentin: What is white outside, green inside, and hops?
Obadiah: I'm in the dark.
Quentin: A frog sandwich.

❐

Fred: What happens if you swallow a frog?
Ted: My mind is blank.
Fred: You'll probably croak any minute.

❐

Gideon: What do you call it when five toads sit on top of each other?
Gloria: You've got me.
Gideon: A toad-em pole.

❒

What happens when frogs get married?
They live hoppily ever after.

❒

Gaylord: What do you say to a hitchhiking frog?
Gladys: You've got me.
Gaylord: Hop in!

❒

Gertrude: What do frogs drink at snack time?
Gerard: I don't have the foggiest.
Gertrude: Croak-a-Cola.

❒

Two frogs were sitting on a lily pad. One leaned over to the other and said, "Time sure is fun when you're having flies."

❒

How do army frogs march?
Hop, two, three, four!

❒

Arnold: Why does a frog have more lives than a cat?
Amy: I have no clue.
Arnold: Because it croaks every night.

❒

Pam: How did you know the frog was sick?
Melba: You've got me.
Pam: He toad me.

❒

Show me a frog on a lily pad, and I'll show you a toadstool.

❒

Q: Where do tadpoles go to change into frogs?
A: The croakroom.

Kermit: What goes, "Tick, tock, croak. Tick, tock, croak?"
Zackery: How should I know?
Kermit: A watch frog.

Gwendolyn: What has big eyes, green skin, and lives alone?
Godfrey: I give up.
Gwendolyn: Hermit the Frog.

Q: When is a frog unable to talk?
A: When he's got a man in his throat.

Fruit

Q: What did the grape say when the elephant stepped on it?
A: Nothing. I just let out a little whine.

What is purple and crazy?
A grape nut.

At what season of the year did Eve eat the fruit?
Early in the fall.

A lady, visiting an orchard, was amazed at the amount of fruit.
"What do you do with all this fruit?" she asked the farmer.
"We eat what we can, and can what we can't," he replied.

Q: How do you get water into watermelons?
A: You plant them in the spring.

What has seeds, a stem, and swings from tree to tree?
Tarzan, King of the Grapes.

□

How do you crush an orange?
Tell it you don't love it anymore.

□

Rudolph: What fruit kept best in Noah's ark?
Thelma: That's a mystery.
Rudolph: The preserved pairs (pears).

□

Abner: What is round and purple, travels in a long, black limousine,
and carries a machine gun?
Agatha: You've got me guessing.
Abner: Al Caplum.

□

Joe: What's the difference between an orange and a yo-yo?
Moe: I don't know.
Joe: You'd be a fine one to send after a dozen oranges!

Furniture

Cecil: What works when it plays, and plays when it works?
Cyrus: I can't guess.
Cecil: A fountain.

□

I have legs, but I can't walk. What am I?
A chair.

□

Antiques: Merchandise sold for old times' sake.

□

I come from a broken home. My kids have broken everything in it.

□

Christy: What is a countryseat?
Lisa: I can't guess.
Christy: A milking stool.

◻

Did you ever see a key punch?

◻

What do you call a girl who likes fine furniture and jewels?
Tiffany.

◻

Quentin: What did the electric plug say to the wall?
Obadiah: I can't guess.
Quentin: Socket to me!

◻

What do you call a girl who gets caught in a fence?
Barb.

◻

Kermit: What is the difference between one yard and two yards?
Zackery: I have no idea.
Kermit: Usually a fence.

G

Games

Cecil: What do they play in Edinburgh when the sidewalks are too hot?
Cyrus: I'm in the dark.
Cecil: Hopscotch!

❏

Q: Why is a crossword puzzle like a quarrel?
A: Because one word leads to another.

❏

Voice on the phone: Is this the game warden?
Game warden: Yes, it is.
Voice: Thank goodness, I have the right person at last. Would you please give me some suggestions for a child's birthday party?

❏

Gertrude: What is a thief's favorite game?
Gerard: That's a mystery.
Gertrude: Hide-n-Sneak.

Garbage Men

"My business is down in the dumps," said the goofy garbage man.

❏

The loony garbage man wrote a novel. It made the best-smellers list.

❏

A garbage truck had a sign: "Always at your Disposal."

❏

Q: What do you get when you cross a gangster and a garbage man?
A: Organized grime.

Gardens

What does a garden say when it laughs?
Hoe, hoe, hoe.

❐

Q: Why is the grass dangerous?
A: Because it's full of blades.

❐

What crime-fighting gardener rides a horse and wears a mask?
The Lawn Ranger.

❐

Q: When is a gardener like a storyteller?
A: When he works up his plot.

❐

Q: Why do gardeners hate weeds?
A: Give weeds an inch and they'll take a yard.

Geese

Gertrude: What kind of geese is found in Portugal?
Gerard: It's unknown to me.
Gertrude: Portu-geese.

❐

What happened when two geese had a head-on collision?
They got goose bumps.

❐

What has four wheels and goes honk?
A goose on a skateboard.

Geography

Why are telephone rates so high in Iran?
Because everyone speaks Persian-to-Persian.

❐

I'm not as stupid as I look. Last week a wise guy tried to sell me the Statue of Liberty and I didn't give him any money—until he gave me a ten-year guarantee on the flame.

❒

Man: I got airsick again last week.
Woman: Oh, were you in an airplane?
Man: No, in Los Angeles.

❒

Where do bacteria go on vacation?
Germany.

❒

How do sailors identify Long Island?
By the Sound.

❒

Gaylord: What state is a number?
Gladys: I have no clue.
Gaylord: Tenn.

❒

What would happen if all the goofy people in Chicago jumped into Lake Michigan?
Lake Michigan would end up with a ring around it.

❒

Gertrude: What Arizona city is named for a banner pole?
Gerard: I don't have a clue.
Gertrude: Flagstaff.

❒

Gwendolyn: What do you get when you cross the United States and the United Kingdom?
Godfrey: My mind is a blank.
Gwendolyn: The Atlantic Ocean.

❒

In a Maine classroom, Miss. Hubbard was telling her pupils how people from different states are given nicknames based on something of significance about their state.

"For example," she explained, "people from North Carolina are called 'Tarheels,' people from Ohio are called 'buckeyes,' and those from Indiana are called 'Hoosiers.' Now, can any of you tell me what they call people from our state of Maine?

Arlene raised her hand. "Maniacs!"

❒

What state was important to Noah?
Ark.

❒

What state is like a piece of clothing?
New Jersey.

❒

Leah: Why does the Statue of Liberty stand in New York Harbor?
Lawrence: That's a mystery.
Leah: Because it can't sit down.

❒

Where do loony bunny rabbits like to spend their vacations?
On Easter Island.

❒

Where do pencils come from?
Pennsylvania.

❒

Teacher: Where's Moscow?
Student: In the barn beside pa's cow.

❒

"I really loved my vacation in California," said the loony lady on the plane to the man sitting next to her.

"Where did you stay?" he asked.

"San Jose."

"Madam, in California we pronounce the J as an H. We say San Hosay. How long were you there?"

"All of Hune and most of Huly."

❒

What city is named after a small stone?
Little Rock, Arkansas.

❒

Derek: What kind of electricity do they use in Washington?
Dorcus: I give up.
Derek: D.C. (direct current).

❒

Q: If all Ireland should sink, what Irish city would remain afloat?
A: Cork.

❒

Eskimo Bill: Where does your mom come from?
Eskimo Bob: Alaska.
Eskimo Bill: Don't bother. I'll ask her myself.

❒

Christy: What is a parasite?
Lisa: You tell me.
Christy: Something you see in Paris.

❒

Cecil: What was the largest island in the world before Australia was discovered?
Cyrus: I give up.
Cecil: Australia.

❒

Ryan: What town doesn't have crime in the streets?
Mark: Beats me.
Ryan: Venice.

❒

Edna: What country is useful at mealtime?
Eldon: How should I know?
Edna: China.

❒

Scotland Yard: Three feet. The same as everywhere else.

❒

Ambrose: What state is round at both ends and high in the middle?
Stella: I'm blank.
Ambrose: Ohio.

◘

Teacher: How do you spell Mississippi?
Willie: The state or the river?

◘

Edna: What state serves as a source of metal?
Eldon: I don't know.
Edna: Ore.

◘

Q: Why are all the Western prairies so flat?
A: Because the sun sets on them every evening.

◘

Leonard: If there is a red house on the right and a blue house on the left, where is the white house?
Leona: Search me.
Leonard: In Washington, D. C.

◘

Quentin: What country has a good appetite?
Obadiah: You've got me.
Quentin: Hungary.

Ghosts

Clem: What is the first thing ghosts do when they get in a car?
Slim: I have no clue.
Clem: They boo-ckle up.

◘

Where do the dead letters go?
To the Ghost Office.

◘

If you were locked in a cemetery at night, how would you get out?
Use a skeleton key.

❏

Cornelius: What's the difference between a ghost and a lame sailor walking?
Henrietta: I don't know.
Cornelius: One is a hobgoblin, and the other is a gob hobblin.

❏

Ryan: What is a haunted wigwam?
Mark: Search me.
Ryan: A creepy teepee.

❏

Ryan: What is a ghoul's favorite food for lunch?
Mark: I pass.
Ryan: Goulash.

❏

Ferdinand: What do ghosts have for dessert?
Gertrude: My mind's a blank.
Ferdinand: Boo-berry pie.

Giraffes

Levi: Why do giraffes have such long necks?
Lois: I'm a blank.
Levi: To connect their heads to their bodies.

❏

Cyrus: What is the highest form of animal life?
Cornelia: I don't know.
Cyrus: A giraffe.

❏

Edna: What do giraffes have that no other animals have?
Eldon: Who knows.
Edna: Little giraffes.

❏

Edna: What is worse than a giraffe with a sore throat?
Eldon: It's unknown to me.
Edna: A centipede with corns.

❐

Lois: Why do giraffes find it difficult to apologize?
Lola: I have no clue.
Lois: It takes them a long time to swallow their pride.

Girlfriends

My girlfriend's so conceited, she goes to the garden to let the flowers smell her.

❐

Dawn: I'm engaged to an Irishman.
Darleen: Oh, really?
Dawn: No, O'Reilly.

❐

Goofy bachelor: Listen, baby, you have to admit that guys like me don't grow on trees.
Girls: No, they swing from them!

❐

She: With stars in her eyes she asked, "Is this a real diamond ring?"
He: It better be, or I've been cheated out of 29 cents.

Goats

Doreen: Why is it hard to carry on a conversation with a goat?
Duncan: My mind is blank.
Doreen: It's always butting in.

❐

Q: How do we know that mountain goats have feet?
A: Because they are sure-footed.

❐

Jack: My roommate makes life unbearable. He keeps six sheep and five goats in the bedroom and it smells terrible.
Mack: Why don't you open the window?
Jack: What, and let all my pigeons escape?

Golf

Christy: Did you hear about the golfer?
Quentin: No, I didn't. What about him?
Christy: He joined a club.

❐

Q: Why can't you drive a golf ball?
A: It doesn't have a steering wheel.

Hair

Q: Why does an Indian wear feathers in his hair?
A: To keep his wigwam.

❏

Patient: How can I avoid falling hair?
Doctor: Step to one side.

❏

Patient: My hair is coming out. What can you give me to keep it in?
Doctor: A cigar box.

❏

Gus: What are the last three hairs on a dog's tail called?
Gabriel: That's a mystery.
Gus: Dog hairs.

❏

Edna: Why did the little girl eat bullets?
Eldon: That's a mystery.
Edna: Because she wanted to grow bangs.

Hands

Arnold: Why did the pinky go to jail?
Amy: Who knows?
Arnold: The police fingered him.

❏

Claud: What did the man get when he dialed 555–273859361394364737 on his phone?
Chloe: I don't know.
Claud: A blister on his finger.

❏

Patient: Should I file my nails?
Doctor: No. Throw them away like everyone else.

❒

Q: When do you have four hands?
A: When you double your fists.

❒

Q: What do you get when you put your hand in a pot?
A: A potted palm.

Heroes

Martyr: A self-made hero.

❒

Q: Why do heroes where big shoes?
A: Because of the amazing feats.

❒

Edna: What would you call Batman and Robin if they were run over by a truck?
Eldon: I don't have the foggiest.
Edna: Flatman and Ribbon.

❒

Gideon: Who does Clark Kent turn into when he is hungry?
Gloria: Beats me.
Gideon: Supperman.

❒

Kermit: What is Batman's favorite sport?
Zackery: I don't have the foggiest.
Kermit: Batminton.

Hippos

Why did the hippo stop using soap?
Because he left a ring around the river.

❒

What is gray and spins around and around?
A hippo stuck in a revolving door.

❐

Jon-Mark: Can you tell me where hippos are found?
Jonas: Hippos are so big they hardly ever get lost.

❐

Bill: Why does a hippopotamus wear glasses?
Jill: That's a mystery.
Bill: So he can read fine print.

❐

Ryan: What do you get if you cross a hippopotamus with a cat?
Reginald: I can't guess.
Ryan: A hippopotamus with nine lives.

❐

What is large and gray and bumps into submarines?
A near-sighted hippo scuba diver.

History

Debby: My ancestors came over on the Mayflower.
Denise: My ancestors came over a month before—on the April Shower.

❐

Calvin: It's Washington's birthday, so I baked you a cherry pie.
Cora: All right, bring me a hatchet so I can cut it.

❐

Ambrose: What did Paul Revere say when he finished his famous ride?
Stella: You tell me.
Ambrose: "Whoa."

❐

What is the difference between Christopher Columbus and the lid of a dish?
One is a discoverer; the other is a dish coverer.

❐

What U.S. president got hit by a truck?
George Squashington.

❒

Who caught flies with his tongue and was the first treasurer of the United States?
Salamander Hamilton.

❒

Show me the first president's dentures, and I'll show you the George Washington Bridge.

❒

Show me where Stalin is buried, and I'll show you a Communist plot.

❒

Calvin: Abraham Lincoln once dined at this very table in my house.
Cora: Is that why you haven't changed the tablecloth since?

❒

Jeff: What did George Washington say to his men before crossing the Delaware?
Joel: I can't guess.
Jeff: Get in the boat.

Hobbies

How does your stamp album feel when it's kept in the refrigerator?
Cool, calm, and collected.

❒

Loony #1: How are you doing with your woodcarving?
Loony #2: It's coming along whittle by whittle.

Hobos

Pam: How does a hobo travel?
Melba: I have no clue.
Pam: On a tramp steamer.

❒

What do they call a loony hobo who has been caught in a pouring rain?
A damp tramp.

Horses

Amount: What a soldier in the cavalry rides.

You tell 'em, horse. You carry a tale.

When does a horse talk?
Whinny wants to.

What was the name of Isaiah's horse?
Is Me. Isaiah said, "Woe, is me."

Pam: How did your horse farm turn out?
Melba: Terrible. I planted the horses too deep.

Ichabod: When is it proper to go to bed with your shoes on?
Eutychus: You've got me.
Ichabod: When you are a horse.

Ichabod: When is a horse not a horse?
Eutychus: That's a mystery.
Ichabod: When he turns into a barn.

Levi: Why did the farmer's horse go over the mountain?
Lois: I don't know.
Levi: He couldn't go under it.

Q: How do you get a horse out of a bathtub?
A: Pull out the plug.

❐

Jeff: What do you call a horse that never stops telling you what to do?
Joel: I have no clue.
Jeff: A real nag.

❐

Q: Why is a horse halfway through a gate like a coin?
A: Because his head's on one side and his tail's on the other.

❐

What do horses do for entertainment?
Watch stable TV.

❐

Q: Why is a horse the most unusual eater of all animals?
A: Because he eats his best when there isn't a bit in his mouth.

❐

Q: Why was the pony called a hothead?
A: Because he had a blaze on his forehead.

Hot Dogs

Peggy: How do hot dogs speak?
Paul: I have no idea.
Peggy: Frankly.

❐

Abner: How did the joker make a hot dog shiver?
Abigail: I can't guess.
Abner: He covered it with chili beans.

❐

Willard: What do you call a hot dog when it's in a bad mood?
Wallace: That's a mystery.
Willard: A crank-furter.

❑

Customer: Give me two hot dogs—one with ketchup, one without.
Dumb waiter: Which one?

❑

How do you make a hot dog stand?
Take away its chair.

Houses

Did you hear about the boardinghouse that blew up?
Roomers were flying.

❑

Did you hear about the loony upside-down lighthouse?
It's for submarines.

❑

Why do you occasionally see loony people pushing a house down the street?
That's how they jump-start their furnaces.

❑

Q: Why was the Swiss yodeler thrown out of the boardinghouse?
A: He owed the old lady!

❑

Farmer: I'd like some 4 by 2's.
Clerk: We only have 2 by 4's.
Farmer: That's okay, we can turn them around.
Clerk: How long do you want them?
Farmer: Oh, we want them for a long time. We're going to build a house.

Hummingbirds

Q: Why does a hummingbird hum?
A: He doesn't know the words.

❐

Geneva: What do you get when you cross a hummingbird with a bell?
Guthrie: You've got me.
Geneva: A humdinger.

I

Ice

What did the iceman say?
Not so hot.

❒

While taking a cruise in the Arctic, Mrs. Cross suddenly pointed across the ocean and said, "Look! An iceberg!"

Mr. Cross looked and looked where she was pointing, but he didn't see a thing.

"Obviously, darling, you have a problem," said Mrs. Cross.

"What problem is that?" he asked.

"Poor ice sight," she replied.

❒

Iceberg: A kind of permanent wave.

❒

No one laughed when I fell on the ice, but the ice made some awful cracks.

Ice Cream

What ice cream do monkeys eat?
Chocolate chimp.

❒

Q: How do you make an elephant float?
A: Two scoops of ice cream, soda, and some elephant!

❒

What do you call an ice cream man in the state of Arizona?
The Good Yuma man.

❒

Rob: Where do you learn how to scoop ice cream?
Rachel: That's a mystery.
Rob: At sundae school.

Illnesses

Q: Why would the jailed man want to catch the measles?
A: So he could break out.

❐

What is the difference between a photocopy machine and the Hong Kong flu?
The one makes facsimiles, the other makes sick families.

❐

Nit: What's red and red and red all over?
Wit: I have no idea.
Nit: Measles with a sunburn.

❐

Which is faster: hot or cold?
Hot is faster. You can catch cold.

❐

Why does a person who is sick lose his sense of touch?
Because he doesn't feel well.

❐

Doctor: I'm afraid there's no cure for your illness.
Patient: I'd like a second opinion.
Doctor: Very well, make an appointment to see me again next week.

❐

Patient: Doctor, nobody can figure out what is wrong with me. I've got the oddest collection of symptoms.
Loony doctor: Have you had it before?
Patient: Yes.
Loony doctor: Well, you've got it again.

❐

Patient: Will my chicken pox be better next week, Doctor?
Doctor: I don't know. I hate to make rash promises.

Insects

What are two of the smallest insects mentioned in the Bible?
The widow's "mites" and the "wicked flee"—Mark 12:42 and Proverbs 28:1.

❐

Jon-Mark: Jonas! What is this fly doing in the alphabet soup you gave me?
Jonas: Learning to read.

❐

Ichabod: Did you ever see a catfish?
Eutychus: No, but I saw a horsefly.

❐

Lynette: What do you call a newborn beetle?
LeRoy: You've got me guessing.
Lynette: A baby buggy!

❐

Q: How do you keep flies out of the kitchen?
A: Keep your garbage can in the living room.

❐

Gertrude: Who has six legs, wears a coonskin cap, and chirps?
Gerard: Beats me.
Gertrude: Davy Cricket.

❐

Gertrude: What singing grasshopper lives in a fireplace?
Gerard: You've got me.
Gertrude: Chimney Cricket.

❐

What nasty bug is responsible for eating up the poor farmer's cotton?
The evil weevil.

❒

What is worse than a centipede with corns?
A hippopotamus with chapped lips.

❒

Archibald: Waiter, there's a fly in my pea soup.
Waiter: There's nothing to worry about, sir. I'll take it back and exchange it for a pea.

❒

Wilber: What kinds of bugs live at the very bottom of the ocean?
Wanda: I don't know.
Wilber: Wet ones.

J

Jobs

Ambrose: What job does a loon do in the forest?
Agatha: Who knows?
Ambrose: He's a loon ranger.

□

Pam: How did the ex-convict get a job at the music store?
Melba: You tell me.
Pam: Not too well, they found out he had a record.

□

Do you know what Mr. Goodyear is doing now?
He is re-tired.

□

Boss: The first thing you should know about the job is it pays $50 a week.
Applicant: Why, that's an insult!
Boss: But we only pay every two weeks, so you're not insulted as often.

□

How did the rocket lose his job?
He was fired.

□

He was so slow that they had to show him how the wastebasket worked the first day on his new job.

□

Loony employer: And you say you've been fired from ten different jobs?
Loony worker: Well, my father always said, "Never be a quitter!"

□

I have a friend who got a job in a drugstore. But he was fired the first day after he told his boss he couldn't get the pill bottles into the typewriter.

❐

Debby: Do you like your job cleaning chimneys?
Denise: It certainly soots me.

❐

Why did the prizefighter like his new job?
He got to punch the time clock.

Jokes

Griff: Have you heard the joke about the big burp?
Gretchen: No.
Griff: Never mind, it's not worth repeating.

❐

I never tell jokes about ceilings because the punch lines always go over everyone's heads.

❐

Fox: Who makes up jokes about knitting?
Owl: A nitwit.

❐

Why did the comedian's wife sue for divorce?
She claimed he was trying to joke her to death.

❐

Did you hear the joke about the mountain climber?
He hasn't made it up yet.

K

Kangaroos

Wilber: What do you get if you cross a kangaroo and an elephant?
Wanda: You tell me.
Wilber: Giant holes all over Australia!

❐

Levi: Why were 1980, 1984, and 1988 good years for kangaroos?
Lois: I have no clue.
Levi: They were leap years.

❐

Doreen: Why did the kangaroo go to the psychiatrist?
Duncan: I have no clue.
Doreen: Because it was jumpy.

Kings

Art: What do you say to a king who falls off his chair?
Bart: I have no clue.
Art: Throne for a loop?

❐

Art: What does a king drink when he doesn't like coffee?
Bart: Who knows?
Art: Royal-tea.

❐

Lola: Where does the king keep his army?
Lionel: That's a mystery.
Lola: Up his sleeve-y.

Kisses

Why is a kiss like gossip?
Because it goes from mouth to mouth.

❐

What adds color and flavor to a very popular pastime?
Lipstick.

❐

He: I understand your kisses speak the language of love.
She: Yes.
He: Well, let's talk things over.

❐

Kiss: Something that is taken at face value.

Knock, Knocks

Knock, knock.
Who's there?
Annie.
Annie who?
Annie body home?

❐

Knock, knock.
Who's there?
Wooden shoe.
Wooden shoe who?
Wooden shoe like to know!

❐

Knock, knock.
Who's there?
Noah.
Noah who?
Noah good knock-knock joke?

❐

Knock, knock.
Who's there?
Catsup.
Catsup who?
Catsup a tree. Quick, call the fire department!

❏

Knock, knock.
Who's there?
Foreign.
Foreign who?
Foreign 20 blackbirds baked in a pie.

❏

Knock, knock.
Who's there?
Cain.
Cain who?
Cain you hear me going knock, knock?

❏

Knock, knock.
Who's there?
Bee Hive.
Bee Hive who?
Bee Hive yourself or you will get into trouble.

❏

Knock, knock.
Who's there?
Pasteur.
Pasteur who?
It's Pasteur bedtime.

❏

Knock, knock.
Who's there?
Wash Out.
Wash Out who?
Wash Out, I'm coming in!

❏

Knock, knock.
Who's there?
Noah.
Noah who?
Noah good place to eat around here?

❐

Knock, knock.
Who's there?
Chester.
Chester who?
Chester minute and I'll see.

❐

Knock, knock.
Who's there?
Osborn.
Osborn who?
Osborn in August.

❐

Knock, knock.
Who's there?
Max.
Max who?
Max no difference. Let me in.

❐

Knock, knock.
Who's there?
Kleenex.
Kleenex who?
Kleenex are prettier than dirty necks.

❐

Knock, knock.
Who's there?
Adore.
Adore who?
Adore is between us. Open up!

❐

Knock, knock.
Who's there?
Waterloo.
Waterloo who?
Waterloo doing for dinner?

Knock, knock.
Who's there?
Hollywood.
Hollywood who?
Hollywood be here if she could!

Knock, knock.
Who's there?
Whittier.
Whittier who?
Whittier people always tell knock-knock jokes!

Knock, knock.
Who's there?
John.
John who?
John your marks, get set, go!

Knock, knock.
Who's there?
Esther.
Esther who?
Esther a doctor in the house?

Knock, knock.
Who's there?
Canoe.
Canoe who?
Canoe come out and play with me?

Knock, knock.
Who's there?
China.
China who?
China cold out, isn't it?

Knock, knock.
Who's there?
Kenya.
Kenya who?
Kenya open the door?

Knock, knock.
Who's there?
Ghana.
Ghana who?
Ghana make you laugh!

Knock, knock.
Who's there?
April.
April who?
April showers.

Knock, knock.
Who's there?
Eric.
Eric who?
Eric conditioner.

Knock, knock.
Who's there?
Witless.
Witless who?
Witless ring I thee wed.

Knock, knock.
Who's there?
You.
You who?
Are you calling me?

□

Knock, knock.
Who's there?
Hugh Maid.
Hugh Maid who?
Hugh Maid your bed, now lie in it!

□

Knock, knock.
Who's there?
Tacoma.
Tacoma who?
Tacoma all this way and you don't recognize me!

□

Knock, knock.
Who's there?
Telly.
Telly who?
Telly scope.

□

Knock, knock.
Who's there?
Moth.
Moth who?
Moth grows on the north side of trees.

□

Knock, knock.
Who's there?
Boo.
Boo who?
Crybaby!

□

Knock, knock.
Who's there?
Hewlett.
Hewlett who?
Hewlett the cat out of the bag?

❐

Knock, knock.
Who's there?
Eyewash.
Eyewash who?
Eyewash I had a million dollars.

❐

Knock, knock.
Who's there?
Stan.
Stan who?
Stan back! I'm coming in.

❐

Knock, knock.
Who's there?
Allacin.
Allacin who?
Allacin Wonderland.

❐

Knock, knock.
Who's there?
Dewey.
Dewey who?
Dewey have to listen to all of this knocking?

❐

Knock, knock.
Who's there?
Wooden.
Wooden who?
Wooden you like to go out with me?

❐

Knock, knock.
Who's there?
Adele.
Adele who?
Adele is where the farmer's in.

Knock, knock.
Who's there?
Caesar.
Caesar who?
Caesar jolly good fellow, Caesar jolly good fellow.

Knock, knock.
Who's there?
Thatcher.
Thatcher who?
Thatcher was a funny joke.

Knock, knock.
Who's there?
Boo-hoo.
Boo-hoo who?
Boo-hoo-hoo.
Boo-hoo-hoo who?
Boo-hoo-hoo-hoo.
Boo-hoo-hoo-hoo who?
Boo-hoo-hoo-hoo-hoo.
Boo-hoo-hoo-hoo-hoo who?
Stop it! You're breaking my heart.

Knock, knock.
Who's there?
Jupiter.
Jupiter who?
Jupiter fly in my soup?

Knock, knock.
Who's there?
Amaryllis.
Amaryllis who?
Amaryllis state agent. Wanna buy a house?

❐

Knock, knock.
Who's there?
Cows go.
Cows go who?
No, cows go "moo."

❐

Knock, knock.
Who's there?
Howell.
Howell who?
Howell I get in if you don't open the door?

❐

Knock, knock.
Who's there?
Abbey.
Abbey who?
Abbey birthday.

❐

Knock, knock.
Who's there?
Freeze.
Freeze who?
Freeze a jolly good fellow…

❐

Knock, knock.
Who's there?
Police.
Police who?
Police stop telling me these nutty knock-knock jokes!

❐

Knock, knock.
Who's there?
Popeye.
Popeye who?
Popeye've got to have the car tonight.

❐

Knock, knock.
Who's there?
Hosea.
Hosea who?
Hosea can you see?

❐

Knock, knock.
Who's there?
Milt.
Milt who?
Milt the cow.

❐

Knock, knock.
Who's there?
Manila.
Manila who?
Manila ice cream!

❐

Knock, knock.
Who's there?
Easter.
Easter who?
Easter anyone home?

❐

Knock, knock.
Who's there?
Luke.
Luke who?
Luke both ways before crossing.

❐

Knock, knock.
Who's there?
Carrie.
Carrie who?
Carrie me inside, I'm tired.

Knock, knock.
Who's there?
Luke.
Luke who?
Luke through the keyhole and see.

Knock, knock.
Who's there?
Ken.
Ken who?
Ken't you guess?

Knock, knock.
Who's there?
Dill.
Dill who?
Big Dill!

Knock, knock.
Who's there?
Archer.
Archer who?
Archer glad to see me?

Knock, knock.
Who's there?
Cologne.
Cologne who?
Cologne Ranger!

Knock, knock.
Who's there?
Yukon.
Yukon who?
Yukon too many people!

Knock, knock.
Who's there?
Amnesia.
Amnesia who?
Oh, I see you have it, too!

Knock, knock.
Who's there?
Canoe.
Canoe who?
Canoe please get off my foot?

Knock, knock.
Who's there?
Tuna.
Tuna who?
Tuna to a disco station!

Knock, knock.
Who's there?
Sarah.
Sarah who?
Sarah echo in here?

Knock, knock.
Who's there?
Saul.
Saul who?
Saul in your head!

Knock, knock.
Who's there?
Lotto.
Lotto who?
Lotto good that will do.

❐

Knock, knock.
Who's there?
Mayonnaise.
Mayonnaise who?
Mayonnaise have seen the glory of the coming of the Lord . . .

❐

Knock, knock.
Who's there?
Hi, this is just Diane.
Just Diane who?
Just Diane to see you.

❐

Knock, knock.
Who's there?
Amarillo.
Amarillo who?
Amarillo-fashioned cowboy.

❐

Knock, knock.
Who's there?
Eskimo, Christian, Italian.
Eskimo, Christian, Italian who?
Eskimo, Christian, Italian no lies.
(Ask me no questions; I'll tell you no lies.)

❐

Knock, knock.
Who's there?
Alby.

Alby who?
Alby glad when school is over.

Knock, knock.
Who's there?
Duncan.
Duncan who?
Duncan doughnuts in your milk makes 'em soft.

Knock, knock.
Who's there?
Amos.
Amos who?
Amos-kito bit me.

Knock, knock.
Who's there?
Andy.
Andy who?
Andy bit me again.

Knock, knock.
Who's there?
Apollo.
Apollo who?
Apollo you anywhere if you'll blow in my ear.

Knock, knock.
Who's there?
Sari.
Sari who?
Sari I was sarong!

Knock, knock.
Who's there?

Ether.
Ether who?
Ether Bunny.

❐

Knock, knock.
Who's there?
Stella.
Stella who?
Stella nother Ether Bunny.

❐

Knock, knock.
Who's there?
Samoa.
Samoa who?
Samoa Ether Bunnies.

❐

Knock, knock.
Who's there?
Desdemona.
Desdemona who?
Desdemona Lisa still hanging on the gallery wall?

❐

Knock, knock.
Who's there?
Jewel.
Jewel who?
Jewel know who when you open the door.

❐

Knock, knock.
Who's there?
Anita Loos.
Anita Loos who?
Anita Loos about 20 pounds.

❐

Knock, knock.
Who's there?
Ghana.
Ghana who?
Ghana wash that man right out of my hair.

Knock, knock.
Who's there?
Gil.
Gil who?
Gil the umpire!

Will you remember me in five years?
Yes.
Will you remember me next year?
Yes.
Will you remember me next month?
Yes.
Will you remember me next week?
Yes.
Will you remember me tomorrow?
Yes.
Will you remember me in another minute?
Yes.
Will you remember me in another second?
Yes.
Knock, knock.
Who's there?
You forgot me already?

Knock, knock.
Who's there?
Dawn.
Dawn who?
Dawnkey, Hee-haw.

Knock, knock.
Who's there?
Uganda.
Uganda who?
Uganda come in without knocking!

❐

Knock, knock.
Who's there?
Hume.
Hume who?
Hume do you expect?

❐

Knock, knock.
Who's there?
Iran.
Iran who?
Iran up the stairs and I'm outta breath.

❐

Knock, knock.
Who's there?
Norma Lee?
Norma Lee who?
Norma Lee we go swimming on Sundays, but I thought we'd see you instead.

❐

Knock, knock.
Who's there?
Diploma.
Diploma who?
Diploma to fix da leak.

❐

Knock, knock.
Who's there?
Sultan.

Sultan who?
Sultan pepper.

Knock, knock.
Who's there?
Yah.
Yah who?
Gosh, I'm glad to see you too!

Knock, knock.
Who's there?
Nana.
Nana who?
Nana your business.

Knock, knock.
Who's there?
Major.
Major who?
Major open the door didn't I?

Knock, knock.
Who's there?
Anita.
Anita who?
Anita minute to think it over.

Knock, knock.
Who's there?
Phyllis.
Phyllis who?
Phyllis in on the news.

Knock, knock.
Who's there?
Tick.
Tick who?
Tick um up. I'm a tongue-tied cowboy.

❐

Knock, knock.
Who's there?
Yukon.
Yukon who?
Yukon say that again.

❐

Knock, knock.
Who's there?
Jess.
Jess who?
Jess little old me.

❐

Knock, knock.
Who's there?
Ooze.
Ooze who?
Ooze in charge around here?

❐

Knock, knock.
Who's there?
Frankfurter.
Frankfurter who?
Frankfurter memories.

❐

Knock, knock.
Who's there?
Shelby.
Shelby who?
Shelby comin' round the mountain when she comes.

❐

Knock, knock.
Who's there?
Distress.
Distress who?
Distress is very short.

❐

Knock, knock.
Who's there?
Sara!
Sara who?
Sara doctor in the house?

❐

Knock, knock.
Who's there?
Adam.
Adam who?
Adam my way, I'm coming in!

❐

Knock, knock.
Who's there?
Kenya.
Kenya who?
Kenya hear me knocking?

❐

Knock, knock?
Who's there?
Midas.
Midas who?
Midas well try again.

❐

Knock, knock.
Who's there?
Fitzby.
Fitzby who?
Fitzby grinning to look a lot like Christmas.

❐

Knock, knock.
Who's there?
Razor.
Razor who?
Razor your hands. This is a stick up.

❏

Knock, knock.
Who's there?
Owl.
Owl who?
Owl aboard.

❏

Knock, knock.
Who's there?
Wendy.
Wendy who?
Wendy joke is over, you had better laugh.

❏

Knock, knock.
Who's there?
Doris.
Doris who?
Doris open. Mind if I come in?

❏

Knock, knock.
Who's there?
Barbara.
Barbara who?
Barbara black sheep, have you any wool?

❏

Knock, knock.
Who's there?
Owl.
Owl who?
Owl be seeing you!

❏

Knock, knock.
Who's there?
Hugo.
Hugo who?
Hugo your way—I'll go mine!

Knock, knock.
Who's there?
Pecan.
Pecan who?
Pecan someone your own size.

Knock, knock.
Who's there?
Omega.
Omega who?
Omega better jokes than these, please!

Knock, knock.
Who's there?
Just a minute and I'll see.

Knock, knock.
Who's there?
Yul.
Yul who?
Yul never know.

Knock, knock.
Who's there?
Hiram.
Hiram who?
Hiram fine. How are you?

Knock, knock.
Who's there?
Warrior.
Warrior who?
Warrior been all my life?

❐

Knock, knock.
Who's there?
Annapolis.
Annapolis who?
Annapolis day keeps the doctor away.

❐

Knock, knock.
Who's there?
Oscar.
Oscar who?
Oscar silly question, get a silly answer!

❐

Knock, knock.
Who's there?
Manuel.
Manuel who?
Manuel be sorry if you don't unlock the door!

❐

Knock, knock.
Who's there?
Arthur.
Arthur who?
Arthur any jobs available?

❐

Knock, knock.
Who's there?
Radio.
Radio who?
Radio not—here I come.

❐

Knock, knock.
Who's there?
Toodle.
Toodle who?
Toodle who to you, too!

Knock, knock.
Who's there?
Barbie.
Barbie who?
Barbie Q Chicken.

Knock, knock.
Who's there?
Noah.
Noah who?
Noah good place to eat?

Knock, knock.
Who's there?
Roach.
Roach who?
Roach you a letter, did you get it?

Knock, knock.
Who's there?
Carmen.
Carmen who?
Carmen to my parlor, said the spider to the fly.

Knock, knock.
Who's there?
Altoona.
Altoona who?
Altoona piano and you play it.

Knock, knock.
Who's there?
House.
House who?
House it going?

Knock, knock.
Who's there?
Lettuce.
Lettuce who?
Lettuce discuss this like mature adults.

Knock, knock.
Who's there?
Albee.
Albee who?
Albee a monkey's uncle!

Knock, knock.
Who's there?
Wanda.
Wanda who?
Wanda come out and play?

L

Landmarks

Rudolph: What is in the Great Wall of China that the Chinese never put there?
Thelma: I have no idea.
Rudolph: Cracks.

❐

Q: Why wasn't the man hurt when he jumped off the Empire State Building?
A: Because he was wearing his light fall suit.

❐

Rudolph: What makes the Tower of Pisa lean?
Thelma: You tell me.
Rudolph: It doesn't eat enough.

Laughs

Ron: Hi, Mom, I'm home.
Mother: Where have you been?
Ron: I had to stay after school again.
Mother: For crying out loud!
Ron: No, for laughing out loud.

❐

Luann: What remedy is there for someone who splits his sides with laughter?
Lowell: Who knows?
Luann: Have him run as fast as he can . . . till he gets a stitch in his side.

❐

Lois: What goes ha-ha-ha-plop?
Lola: It's unknown to me.
Lois: Someone who laughs his head off.

❐

Ryan: What is a tiny laugh in Indian language?
Mark: I have no clue.
Ryan: A Minnehaha.

Lawyers

Lynette: What is the difference between one lawyer in a small town
and two lawyers in a small town?
LeRoy: I have no clue.
Lynette: One can earn an okay living, but two can make a fortune.

❐

Gustave: What do attorneys wear to work?
Gilberta: It's unknown to me.
Gustave: Lawsuits.

❐

Q: Why are lawyers like crows?
A: Because they like to have their caws (cause) heard.

Legs

Kermit: What two animals go with you everywhere?
Zackery: Beats me.
Kermit: Your calves.

❐

Barnaby: Why do people stand on two legs?
Barbie: I have no clue.
Barnaby: If they didn't, they would fall over.

❐

Q: Have you heard about the man with five legs?
A: His trousers fit him like a glove.

Leopards

Eileen: How did you find the lost leopard?
Olivia: I just spotted him.

Levi: Why are leopards spotted?
Lois: It's unknown to me.
Levi: So you can tell them from fleas.

How can a leopard change his spots?
By moving.

Ambrose: What did the leopard say after he ate a hot dog?
Stella: I don't have the foggiest.
Ambrose: That just hit the spot.

Letters

Gustave: Why is it bad to write a letter on an empty stomach?
Gilberta: I can't guess.
Gustave: Because it's much better to write on paper.

Q: Why was the letter so damp?
A: It had postage dew.

Convict: Writing your memoirs?
Cellmate: No, just a letter to myself so I'll get some mail.
Convict: What are you saying?
Cellmate: Don't know. Mail call isn't until 3:30.

What do you call a lady letter carrier?
A mail female.

Edna: What letter is not found in the alphabet?
Eldon: I'm in the dark.
Edna: The one in your mail.

❐

What do you call mail sent to a cat?
Kitty letter.

❐

Boss: Did you put those circulars in the mail?
Secretary: No, sir. I couldn't find any round envelopes for them.

❐

What do you call a guy who delivers the mail?
Bill.

❐

Father: Now I want to put a little scientific question to you, my son. When the kettle boils, what does the steam come out of the spout for?
Son: So that mother can open your letters before you get them.

❐

Doreen: Why does that letter bring tears to your eyes?
Duncan: Search me.
Doreen: It's written on onionskin.

Life

Molly: What nationality are you?
Polly: Well, my father was born in Iceland and my mother was born in Cuba.
Molly: Oh, so you're an Ice Cube?

❐

Mr. Green: Why, when I first came to this city, I was jobless, penniless, shoeless, and without a shred of clothing!
Interviewer: You mean . . .
Mr. Green: That's right! I was born here!

❐

Q: If a man were born in France, raised in Italy, came to America, and died in Los Angeles, what is he?
A: Dead.

❐

Jack: I was born in vain.
Mike: That's funny. I was born in Ohio.

❐

At what time of day was Adam born?
A little before Eve.

❐

What man in the Bible spoke when he was a very small baby?
Job. He cursed the day he was born.

Light Bulbs

Why hasn't someone invented black light bulbs for people who want to read in the dark?

❐

Lana: How many members of the Loony family does it take to screw in a light bulb?
Lark: What's a light bulb?

❐

Lana: How many loony mothers does it take to screw in a light bulb?
Lark: You've got me.
Lana: None. It's all right; I'll just sit here in the dark.

❐

Leah: How many loony psychiatrists does it take to screw in a light bulb?
Lawrence: You've got me.
Leah: Only one—but the light bulb really has to want to change.

❐

Lana: How many loony terrorists does it take to screw in a light bulb?
Lark: I can't guess.
Lana: One hundred. One to screw it in and 99 to hold the house hostage.

❐

How many Californians does it take to change a light bulb?
None. Californians don't put in light bulbs; they put in hot tubs.

❐

How many evolutionists does it take to change a light bulb?
Only one, but it takes him eight million years.

Lions

Q: What do you get when you cross a lion and a monkey?
A: A swinging lion.

❐

Carter: I once shot a lion 15 feet long.
Clara: Some lying!

❐

Cyrus: What makes more noise than an angry lion?
Cornelia: Search me.
Cyrus: Two angry lions.

❐

Gideon: What big cat lives in people's backyards?
Gloria: I don't have a clue.
Gideon: A clothes lion.

❐

How do you stop a charging lion?
Take away his credit cards.

❐

Geraldine: Why do lions roar?
Gaspar: I have no idea.
Geraldine: They would feel silly saying oink, oink.

◻

Debby: What do they call the man who cuts the lion's hair?
Denise: I have no clue.
Debby: The mane man.

◻

Kathy: One time a big lion appeared in front of me.
Ralph: What did you do?
Kathy: I moved to the next cage.

◻

When is it safe to pet a lion?
When it is a dandelion.

◻

Caller: Hello, operator, I would like to speak to the king of the jungle.
Operator: I'm very sorry. The lion is busy.

◻

What do you call a guy who's been attacked by a lion?
Claude.

Lobsters

Eileen: How can you tell if a lobster is fresh?
Olivia: I can't guess.
Eileen: If he tries to kiss you.

◻

Diner: Do you have lobster tails?
Loony waiter: Certainly, sir: Once upon a time, there was a little lobster . . .

Lone Ranger

Fred: What does the Lone Ranger's horse eat with?
Ted: Beats me.
Fred: Silverware.

❏

Lana: If a king sits on the gold, who sits on the silver?
Lark: I don't have the foggiest.
Lana: The Lone Ranger.

❏

Leah: Where does the Lone Ranger take his garbage?
Lawrence: How should I know?
Leah: To the dump, to the dump, to the dump, dump, dump.

Lost & Found

Q: Why should you go to an ironworks to find something you've lost?
A: Because it's a foundry.

❏

Q: Why is it that when you are looking for something, you always find it in the last place you look?
A: Because you always stop looking when you find it.

Love

Eskimo boy: I'd push my dog team through a thousand miles of ice and snow to tell you I love you.
Eskimo girl: That's a lot of mush!

❏

Cindy: Do you see that boy over there annoying Sue?
Frank: Sure, but he isn't even talking to her.
Cindy: That's what's annoying her.

❏

Lady visitor: What a beautiful mountain! There must be many romantic stories connected with it.

Mountaineer: Yep, two lovers went up that mountain and never came back here.

Lady visitor: My, my, what ever became of them?

Mountaineer: Went down the other side.

Luck

Q: Why would you iron a four-leaf clover?
A: To press your luck!

❏

Rufus: What did the joker get when he crossed poison ivy with a four-leaf clover?

Rachel: I don't know.

Rufus: A rash of good luck.

❏

Ferdinand: What do you get if you cross poison ivy with a black cat?

Gertrude: I'm in the dark.

Ferdinand: A rash of bad luck!

❏

I once bought a rabbit's foot for good luck. It kicked me.

❏

Her luck was so bad that her contacts got cataracts.

M

Manners

Jon-Mark: Jonas, your hands are very dirty. What would you say if I came to your house with dirty hands?
Jonas: I'd be too polite to mention it.

❐

Calvin: I wrote a letter to Dear Abby. This is what I said—"Dear Abby: Is it good manners to answer a question with just a single word? Signed, Polite."
Cora: Did she write back?
Calvin: Yes. This is what she said to me—"Dear Polite: No."

Marriage

Mrs. Simple: Did you hear what Cindy Simple's friends did before her wedding?
Mr. Simple: No, what?
Mrs. Simple: Instead of giving her a shower, they made her take one.

❐

Barnaby: Why did the two fish get married?
Barbie: Beats me.
Barnaby: Because they were hooked on each other.

❐

Luann: Who is married to an Egyptian daddy?
Lowell: I give up.
Luann: An Egyptian mummy.

❐

If your aunt ran off to get married, what would you call her?
Antelope.

❐

Lynette: Which state produces the most marriages?
LeRoy: I give up.
Lynette: The state of matrimony.

❐

What state is the same as an unmarried woman?
Miss.

❐

Did you know that Nancy married a janitor?
He just swept her off her feet.

❐

Q: If Mother Goose married Paul Berry, what would be her name?
A: Mother Goose Berry.

❐

Girl: I wouldn't marry you if you were the last person on earth.
Boy: If I were, you wouldn't be here!

❐

Did you hear about the two cement mixers that got married? Now they have a little sidewalk running around their house.

❐

When one hypochondriac married another hypochondriac, the couple exchanged vows and symptoms.

❐

There was a young man and a young woman eloping. They were in a taxi heading for a Justice of the Peace. When they arrived, the young man asked the taxi driver how much the fare was. "No fee," answered the driver. "Her father paid for it."

❐

Q: If a millionaire married a beggar lady, what would the millionaire be?
A: Her husband, of course.

❐

A little girl, sitting in church watching a wedding, suddenly exclaimed: "Mummy, has the lady changed her mind?"

"What do you mean?" the mother asked.

"Why," replied the child, "she went up the aisle with one man and came back with another."

Math

Phil: Do you know what happened to the plant in the math class?
Bill: No, what?
Phil: It grew square roots.

❐

Circle: A round straight line with a hole in the middle.

❐

Leah: What is round and dangerous?
Lawrence: Beats me.
Leah: A vicious circle.

❐

Billy: How many sides does a circle have?
Willie: Two—the inside and the outside.

❐

Loony teacher: If you took three apples from a basket that contained 13 apples, how many apples would you have?
Loony student: If you took three apples, you'd have three apples.

❐

What was the difference between the 10,000 soldiers of Israel and the 300 soldiers Gideon chose for battle?
9,700.

❐

Edgar: What is the best way to find a math tutor?
Emily: I give up.
Edgar: Place an add.

❐

Jeff: What happened on the Fourth of July?
Joel: That's a mystery.
Jeff: I don't know. I'm not good at fractions.

❐

Where is the second math problem mentioned in the Bible?
When God told Adam and Eve to go forth and multiply—Genesis 1:28.

❐

Where is the first math problem mentioned in the Bible?
When God divided the light from the darkness—Genesis 1:4.

❐

Rex: What part of the Bible do people who love math read?
Tex: I don't know.
Rex: The book of Numbers.

❐

What increases in value by half when you turn it upside down?
The number 6.

❐

Gaylord: Why couldn't the geometry teacher walk?
Gladys: I have no idea.
Gaylord: He had a sprained angle.

❐

What is gross stupidity?
One hundred and forty-four goofy people.

❐

It takes 12 one-cent stamps to make a dozen. How many six-cent stamps does it take to make a dozen?
It takes 12 of anything to make a dozen—even six-cent stamps.

❐

Leah: When does 10 plus 7 equal 13?
Lawrence: Search me.
Leah: When you add wrong.

□

Leonard: If two is a company and three is a crowd, what are four and five?
Leona: Who knows?
Leonard: Nine.

□

Ann: I spent ten hours over my math book last night.
Bill: You did?
Ann: Yes, it fell under my bed.

□

Teacher: Are you good at arithmetic?
Student: Yes and no.
Teacher: What does that mean?
Student: Yes, I'm no good at arithmetic.

□

Teacher: If I give you five goldfish today and seven goldfish tomorrow, how many will you have?
Susie: Fourteen.
Teacher: How do you figure that?
Susie: I already have two goldfish.

□

Teacher: How many feet are there in a yard?
Student: Well, it depends on how many people there are.

□

Clem: What can be right but never wrong?
Slim: I have no clue.
Clem: An angle.

□

Kermit: What's the longest piece of furniture in the world?
Zackery: I'm blank.
Kermit: The multiplication table.

Meals

What constitutes a traditional goofy seven-course dinner?
A can of sardines and a six-pack of soda pop.

❒

If you were invited out to dinner and saw nothing but a beet on your plate, what would you say?
That beet's all!

❒

Loony mother: Leslie, will you help me fix dinner?
Loony Leslie: I didn't know it was broken.

❒

Derek: What did the fat man say when he sat down to dinner?
Dorcus: It's unknown to me.
Derek: I'm afraid this food is going to waist.

❒

Gaylord: Who delivers breakfast, lunch, and dinner, and always completes his appointed rounds?
Gladys: Beats me.
Gaylord: The mealman.

❒

"Oh no," the waiter exclaimed when he dropped the Thanksgiving dinner. "This means the fall of Turkey, the ruin of Greece, and the breakup of China."

❒

I once ate in a goofy restaurant that was so bad I got food poisoning just from opening the menu.

❒

How do you make a loony shish kebab?
Shoot an arrow into a garbage can.

❑

Diner: Waiter, where should we sit to be served quickly?
Waiter: How about the restaurant next door?

❑

Quentin: What is it that everybody wants, yet wants to get rid of as soon as possible?
Obadiah: Who knows?
Quentin: A good appetite.

❑

Who was the first person in the Bible to eat herself out of house and home?
Eve.

❑

Say, did you read in the newspaper about the fellow that ate six dozen pancakes at one sitting?
No! How waffle!

❑

What was the most expensive meal served in the Bible, and who ate it?
Esau. It cost him his birthright—Genesis 25:34.

Meat

Q: When is a cigar like dried beef?
A: When it is smoked.

❑

Q: Why is a karate blow like a piece of meat?
A: Because it is a poke chop.

❑

Cecil: What food is dear at any price?
Cyrus: You've got me.
Cecil: Venison.

❏

Fred: What is the best way to introduce a hamburger?
Ted: I have no clue.
Fred: Meat Patty.

❏

Show me a stolen sausage, and I'll show you a missing link.

❏

How many hamburgers can you eat on an empty stomach?
Only one, because after that your stomach is no longer empty.

❏

Q: If hamburgers grew on trees, what would they be called?
A: Limburgers.

❏

What do you call a girl who makes hamburgers?
Patti.

❏

Cecil: What did the steak say to the plate?
Cyrus: I don't know.
Cecil: Pleased to meat you.

❏

Ryan: What do you call a sunburn on your stomach?
Mark: I'm blank.
Ryan: Pot roast.

❏

Diner: Waiter! This London broil tastes like asphalt shingle!
Waiter: Sorry, sir. Meat prices have simply gone through the roof.

❏

Diner: Waiter, this steak is rare. Didn't you hear me say "well done"?
Loony waiter: Yes, sir. Thank you, sir!

❐

When you order bison steaks at a restaurant, what does the waiter bring you after the meal?
A Buffalo Bill.

❐

Rex: What do you say to a liar at the dinner table?
Tex: I have no idea.
Rex: Pass the baloney.

Medicine

Where is medicine first mentioned in the Bible?
Where the Lord gives Moses two tablets.

❐

Patient: Doctor, my child just swallowed a dozen aspirin. What should I do?
Loony doctor: Give him a headache.

❐

Ambrose: What is white and lifts weights?
Agatha: I have no idea.
Ambrose: An extra-strength aspirin.

Mice

Rufus: What is gray, has four legs, and weighs 98 pounds?
Rachel: You've got me.
Rufus: A fat mouse.

❐

What mouse heads the House of Representatives?
The Squeaker of the House.

❐

Ichabod: Tell me, did you ever see the Catskill Mountains?
Eutychus: No, I haven't, but I've seen them kill mice.

Rufus: What is an important aid in good grooming for pet mice?
Rachel: I have no clue.
Rufus: Mouse wash.

Gideon: What is a mouse's favorite game?
Gloria: Tell me.
Gideon: Hide-n-squeak.

Gus: Who is the nastiest Disney character?
Gabriel: Beats me.
Gus: Meanie Mouse.

Christy: What should you do if you woke up in the night and heard a mouse squeaking?
Lisa: I don't know.
Christy: Oil it!

Derek: What are the coldest animals?
Dorcus: Search me.
Derek: Mice, because they are three parts ice.

The other night a Chicken Delight truck came to the door. I went to answer it, but a mouse pushed me aside and said, "That's for me."

How did the mouse pass its exam?
It just squeaked by.

Q: When does a mouse weigh as much as an elephant?
A: When the scale is broken.

The food in our school cafeteria is so bad that last night they caught a mouse trying to phone out for pizza.

Military

Christy: What is the best form for a soldier?
Lisa: I have no idea.
Christy: A uniform.

❐

What is a group of loony paratroopers called?
Air pollution.

❐

What do you call a man walking around with his hands in the air and waving a white flag?
A loony soldier on war maneuvers.

❐

Did you hear about the investigator who joined the army?
He was a private eye.

Milk

Q: When is a pint of milk not a pint?
A: When it's condensed.

❐

Derek: What turns without moving?
Dorcus: Who knows?
Derek: Milk. It can turn sour.

❐

Luther: What should you buy if you want to carry milk around on your wrist?
Lydia: I don't know.
Luther: A quartz watch.

Ministers

Q: Why is a clergyman like a shoemaker?
A: Both try to save soles.

❐

Who can stay single even if he marries many women?
A minister.

❐

An elderly woman was sitting on a plane and getting increasingly nervous about the thunderstorm raging outside. She turned to a minister who was sitting next to her: "Reverend, you are a man of God. Why can't you do something about this problem?"

The loony minister replied: "Lady, I'm in sales, not management."

❐

Gideon: What is a minister doing when he rehearses his sermon?
Gloria: I give up.
Gideon: Practicing what he preaches.

Mirrors

When can you see yourself in a place you've never been?
When you look into a mirror.

❐

Gaylord: What always speaks the truth but doesn't say a word?
Gladys: I don't have the foggiest.
Gaylord: A mirror.

❐

Q: When is a girl like a mirror?
A: When she is a good-looking lass.

❐

Q: I show a different face to everyone, but I have no face of my own. Who am I?
A: A mirror.

Miscellaneous

Edgar: How is the monogram business you started?
Emily: I've had some initial success.

❐

Bertram: What do you say to curtains?
Bernard: That's a mystery.
Bertram: Pull yourself together.

❐

What kind of robbery may not be dangerous?
A safe robbery.

❐

Gertrude: What is easier to give than receive?
Gerard: You tell me.
Gertrude: Criticism.

❐

His favorite pastime is sitting on the sidewalk and watching cement harden.

❐

Rudolph: What is a twip?
Thelma: Search me.
Rudolph: A twip is what a wabbit takes when he wides a too-too twain.

❐

The only reason some people are lost in thought is that they're total strangers there.

❐

Jon-Mark: You mean to tell me that you've lived in this out-of-the-way town for more than 25 years? I can't see what there is here to keep you busy.
Jonas: There isn't anything to keep me busy. That's why I like it!

❐

Map: Something that will tell you everything except how to fold it up again.

□

What do they call a towel that you look at but never use?
A guest towel.

□

When is an elevator not an elevator?
When it's going down.

□

Where do you buy laundry detergent?
In a soapermarket.

□

What word do most people like best?
The last.

□

Gus: Why did the paintbrush retire?
Gabriel: I can't guess.
Gus: It had a stroke.

□

Gwen: So, you are expecting your seventh child! What do you think you'll call it?
Gina: I think I'll call it quits!

□

Gaylord: What do you say to Amillion when he does you a good turn?
Gladys: That's a mystery.
Gaylord: Thanks, Amillion.

□

How did the jewel thief wake up every morning?
To a burglar alarm.

□

Where can you find the finest basements?
On the best-cellar list.

□

When you fill me up, I still look empty. What am I?
A balloon.

□

Did you hear about the goofy man who willed his body to science?
Science is contesting the will.

□

Teacher: What is a leading cause of dry skin?
Student: Towels.

□

Why can't the world ever come to an end?
Because it's round.

□

Luann: What word is always pronounced wrong?
Lowell: You've got me.
Luann: Wrong.

□

Lois: What is the best thing to do if you are going to be beheaded?
Lola: I don't have the foggiest.
Lois: Stay calm and try not to lose your head.

□

Lois: What kind of saw lives in the sea?
Lola: Beats me.
Lois: A seesaw.

□

Lois: What is an anonymous story?
Lola: I can't guess.
Lois: Unauthorized.

□

Lois: What shall we do if Amos acts silly?
Lola: I have no idea.
Lois: Ignoramus.

□

Cost plus: Expensive.

□

Flashlight: A case to carry dead batteries in.

□

Stationary store: A store that stays pretty much at the same location.

□

Lila: What color is a hiccup?
Lillian: I pass.
Lila: Burple.

□

Lila: What is the longest sentence in the world?
Lillian: How should I know?
Lila: Life in prison.

□

Lila: What should you do when your nick is ripe?
Lillian: My mind is a blank.
Lila: Picnic.

□

What do you call two convicts who become buddies in jail?
Pen pals.

□

Lynette: Why does a little boy look one way and then the other way before crossing the street?
LeRoy: You tell me.
Lynette: Because he can't look both ways at the same time.

□

Laurel: What should you do if you feel strongly about graffiti?
LaVonne: I'm in the dark.
Laurel: Sign a partition.

❒

Laurel: What did Mrs. Bullet say to Mr. Bullet?
LaVonne: I don't know.
Laurel: Darling, I'm going to have a BB!

❒

I have wings, but I can't fly. What am I?
A large mansion.

❒

We have only two loony things to worry about—one, that things will never get back to normal, and two, that they already have.

❒

He is so loony that if his looniness were gold, he would be Fort Knox.

❒

Leah: How do batteries get sick?
Lawrence: I don't know.
Leah: They get acid indigestion.

❒

How do you get a one-armed loony man out of a tree?
Wave.

❒

Did you hear about the loony man who locked his keys in the car? It took him nine hours to get his family out.

❒

If a loony man and a loony woman jumped off a 40-story building, which would land first?
The loony man. The loony woman would have to stop and ask for directions.

❒

Did you hear about the loony gift-wrapped empty boxes? They are to give as presents to people who say, "I don't need anything."

□

When does it get noisy in a magazine store?
When Time marches on.

□

Loony boss: You are recommending Jack for a raise? I can't believe it—he's the laziest worker on the line!
Loony foreman: Yes, but his snoring keeps the other workers awake!

□

Who said, "Will you please join me?"
A person who was coming apart.

□

Loony customer: Does the manager know you knocked over this whole pile of canned tomatoes?
Loony stock boy: I think so. He's underneath.

□

Loony Lenora: Did you hear about the man who bought a new pair of snow tire?
Loony Leonard: No, what happened?
Loony Lenora: They melted before he got home.

□

What has a foot at each end and a foot in the middle?
A yardstick.

□

What should you do if you accidentally eat some microfilm?
Wait and see what develops.

□

What is the difference between a man going up the stairs and a man looking up the stairs?
One steps up the stairs, and the other stares up the steps.

□

What did the prisoner say when he bumped into the governor?
Pardon me!

❏

I really like New Year's Day. It's the only day of the year that I'm not behind in my homework.

❏

Q: Can you name a carpenter's tool you can spell forward and backward the same way?
A: Level.

❏

There were three dry-cleaning stores on one block in a big city, and the competition for business was quite fierce. At last, one of the stores put up a big sign in the window: "Best Dry-Cleaners in the City."

About a week later, the second store blossomed forth with a bigger sign: "Best Dry-Cleaners in the World."

And a week after that, the third store put up a modest little sign: "Best Dry-Cleaners on the Block."

❏

Sadie: How can you put yourself through a keyhole?
Madie: How?
Sadie: Write yourself on a piece of paper and push it through.

❏

Mike: How much is 5q plus 5q?
Ike: 10q.
Mike: You're welcome.

❏

Q: How did the man feel when he got his electric bill?
A: He was shocked.

❏

Cornelius: What criminal doesn't take a bath?
Henrietta: I have no idea.
Cornelius: A dirty crook.

❏

Mary: Excuse me. I think you are sitting in my seat.
Big bully: Oh yeah! Can you prove it?
Mary: I think so. I left a lemon meringue pie on it.

❏

Jones: Do you believe in free speech?
Smith: Certainly!
Jones: Splendid! May I use your telephone?

❏

Q: If joy is the opposite of sorrow, what is the opposite of woe?
A: Giddyap.

❏

Rick: Haven't you ever heard of the fall of Rome?
Mick: No, but I remember hearing something drop.

❏

Nick: Look, I've got a new pack of jumbo-sized cards.
Rick: Big deal!

❏

Did you hear about my neighbor who has a sign in his garage? It reads: "Anyone is welcome to use my lawnmower . . . as long as he doesn't take it out of the yard."

❏

Speaker: I want land reform . . . I want housing reform . . . I want educational reform . . . I want . . .
Listener: Chloroform.

❏

Cornelius: What can you put in a glass bottle, but never take out?
Henrietta: I don't know.
Cornelius: A crack.

❏

Dan: Why'd you tell everyone I'm stupid?
Don: I didn't know it was a secret.

❏

Ever notice that the people who say, "That's the way the ball bounces" are usually the ones who dropped it?

❐

Q: Why can one never starve in a desert?
A: Because of the sand which is there.

❐

Q: Why did the robot go mad?
A: Because he had a screw loose.

❐

Q: Why did the projector blush?
A: It saw a film strip.

❐

Derek: What did the man do when he received a big gas bill?
Dorcus: You tell me.
Derek: He exploded.

❐

Derek: What kind of paper makes you itch?
Dorcus: You've got me.
Derek: Scratch paper.

❐

Christy: What can you break without touching it?
Lisa: I don't know.
Christy: Your promise.

❐

Anna: Why did Linda take a hammer to bed with her?
Diane: I don't know. Why?
Anna: So she could hit the hay.

❐

Q: In what month do girls talk the least?
A: February.

❐

Snob: My ancestors came over on the Mayflower.
Slob: That was lucky for them. Immigration laws are stricter now.

❐

Maybe the grass looks greener on the other side of the fence because they take care of it over there.

❐

Ryan: What is very light but can't be lifted?
Mark: I can't guess.
Ryan: A bubble.

❐

Fox: Who was the biggest bandit in history?
Owl: Atlas. He held up the world.

❐

Q: Which Indian was in charge of facial tissue?
A: The hankie-chief.

❐

Husband (looking up from his newspaper): There's a story here that says there's a man run over on New York City streets every eight minutes.
Wife: That's awful. Someone should tell him to stay on the sidewalk.

❐

Boss: An hour late again! What's your excuse this time?
Barney: I was sideswiped by a cross-town bus!
Boss: And I suppose you're going to tell me that took an hour?

❐

Q: Why are country people smarter than city people?
A: The population is denser in the big cities.

❐

Q: Why can't you keep secrets in a bank?
A: Because of all the tellers.

❐

Wilber: What nation always wins in the end?
Wanda: I have no clue.
Wilber: Determi-nation.

◘

Wilber: What did the rake say to the hoe?
Wanda: Beats me.
Wilber: Hi, hoe!

◘

Wilber: What can you make that no one can see?
Wanda: Who knows?
Wilber: A noise.

◘

Rudolph: What is a ringleader?
Thelma: I don't know.
Rudolph: The first person in the bathtub.

◘

Paralyze (PAR-a-lyze): Two untruths.

◘

Don: Stop acting like a moron.
Dan: I'm not acting.

◘

Abner: What is the difference between a church bell and a thief?
Agatha: Beats me.
Abner: One peals from the steeple, and the other steals from the people.

◘

Rudolph: What is blind itself, yet guides the blind?
Thelma: I don't know.
Rudolph: A walking stick.

◘

Rudolph: What is the difference between a greedy person and an electric toaster?
Thelma: I give up.
Rudolph: One takes the most, and the other makes the toast.

❐

Abner: What can speak in every language but never went to school?
Agatha: How should I know?
Abner: An echo.

❐

Ambrose: What would happen if a girl should swallow her teaspoon?
Stella: That's a mystery.
Ambrose: She wouldn't be able to stir.

❐

Cecil: What are the three most common causes of forest fires?
Cyrus: My mind's a blank.
Cecil: Men, women, and children.

❐

Q: How can one tell the naked truth?
A: Just by telling the bare facts.

Moles

What do you get if you hit a gopher with a golf ball?
A mole-in-one.

❐

Cornelius: What travels underground at 80 miles an hour?
Henrietta: I pass.
Cornelius: A mole on a motorbike.

❐

Q: What do you get when you cross a porcupine with a mole?
A: A tunnel that leaks.

Money

What do you call a girl whom you can't seem to get rid of and keeps coming back?

Penny.

❐

Loony speaker: A horrible thing has happened. I've just lost my wallet with $500 in it. I'll give $50 to anyone who will return it.

Loony voice from the rear: I'll give $100.

❐

The boss was watching his new employee count out the day's receipts and asked the man where he got his financial training.

"Yale," he answered.

"Good. And what is your name?"

"Yackson."

❐

When the May Day parade was still a big deal in Moscow, a Westerner noted a phalanx of goofy Soviet economists marching between military units.

"Why are the goofy economists marching in ranks with the army?" the Westerner asked then-President Leonid I. Brezhnev.

"You'd be surprised at the damage they do," said the president.

❐

You tell 'em, cashier. I'm a poor teller.

❐

Who was the best financier in the Bible?

Noah. He floated his stock while the whole world was in liquidation.

❐

What are the only wages that do not have any deductions?

The wages of sin.

❐

Peggy: How would you punctuate the sentence: "I saw a five-dollar bill on the sidewalk"?
Paul: My mind is blank.
Peggy: I'd make a dash after it.

❏

How were Adam and Eve prevented from gambling?
Their pair-o-dice was taken away from them.

❏

How were the Egyptians paid for goods taken by the Israelites when they fled from Egypt?
The Egyptians got a check on the bank of the Red Sea.

❏

When is high finance first mentioned in the Bible?
When Pharaoh's daughter took a little prophet from the bulrushes.

❏

Where is the capital of the United States?
All over the world.

❏

What is the surest way to double your money?
Fold it.

❏

Why should you borrow money from a pessimist?
Because he never expects to get it back.

❏

An angry loony worker went into her company's payroll office to complain that her paycheck was $50 short.

The payroll supervisor checked the books and said, "I see here that last week you were overpaid $50. I can't recall your complaining about that."

"Well, I'm willing to overlook an occasional error, but this is two in a row," said the loony worker.

❏

Q: When does it rain money?
A: Whenever there's a change in the weather.

❐

Fortune-teller: I see great disappointment for someone close to you.
Customer: That's right. I've no money to pay you.

❐

Peggy: How did the dove save so much money?
Paul: I give up.
Peggy: By using coo-pons.

❐

Lola: Where does a track star keep his money?
Lionel: You've got me.
Lola: In a pole vault.

❐

Where do you think the Israelites may have deposited their money?
At the banks of the Jordan.

❐

Was there any money on Noah's ark?
Yes. The duck took a bill, the frog took a greenback, and the skunk took a scent.

❐

Where is one place you can always find money?
In the dictionary, of course!

❐

Betty: I wish I had enough money to buy an elephant.
Billy: Why on earth do you want an elephant?
Betty: I don't. I just want the money.

❐

Laurel: Where do Eskimos keep their money?
LaVonne: I can't guess.
Laurel: In a snow bank.

❐

Once upon a time there were three men on their way home from work. The first man, passing a deserted shack, saw a ten-dollar bill on the ground. He was about to pick it up when he heard a voice say, "This is the voice of Daniel Boone. Touch that money, and it'll be your doom."

The man left the money and ran away.

The second man came by, heard the voice, and he, too, ran away.

Then the third man walked past. He picked up the money, and the voice said, "This is the voice of Daniel Boone. Touch that money, and it'll be your doom."

The third man said, "This is the voice of Davy Crockett. This ten-dollar bill goes in my pocket!"

❏

I think our currency is headed for another fall on the world market. Yesterday, I looked at a five-dollar bill and Abraham Lincoln was wearing a crash helmet.

❏

Patient: Doctor, what's the difference between an itch and an allergy?
Loony doctor: About $35.

❏

What is the difference between an 11-year-old girl and a 15-year-old girl?

A $5 difference in your phone bill.

❏

Customer: How much are these oranges?
Grocer: Two for a quarter.
Customer: How much is just one?
Grocer: Fifteen cents.
Customer: Then I'll take the other one.

❏

Voice on the phone: Is this Joe?
Joe: Sure, this is Joe.
Caller: Doesn't sound like Joe.
Joe: It's Joe, all right.
Caller: Can you loan me $10, Joe?
Joe: I'll ask him as soon as he comes in.

❏

Three men in a dining compartment of a train were discussing the vagaries of men. One said, "I know a man who writes very small hand to save ink."

Another said, "A friend of my father always stops the clock at night to save wear and tear on it."

"Your men are spendthrifts," said the third. "I know an old man who won't read the paper because, he says, it wears out his glasses."

❏

Today, carsickness is what you get from looking at the sticker price.

❏

An auction is a place where you can get something for nodding.

❏

Q: Do you know why Robin Hood robbed only the rich?
A: Poor people don't have any money.

Monkeys

Jeff: What kind of monkey flies?
Joel: I give up.
Jeff: A hot-air baboon.

❏

Who was the first man to make a monkey of himself?
Darwin.

❏

What happens when a chimpanzee twists his ankle?
He gets a monkey wrench.

❏

Gus: What does the government use when it takes a census of all the monkeys in the zoos?
Gabriel: My mind is a blank.
Gus: An ape recorder.

❏

Q: How did the chimpanzee get out of his cage?
A: He used a monkey wrench.

Monsters

Fox: Who brings the monster's babies?
Owl: Frankenstork.

❐

Show me a pharaoh who ate crackers in bed, and I'll show you a crummy mummy.

❐

Derek: What instrument do you use to see monsters?
Dorcus: How should I know?
Derek: A horror-scope.

❐

How do you make a Big Mac monster burger?
You put two people patties, special sauce, lettuce, cheese, pickles, and onions on a sesame seed bun.

❐

Q: Why couldn't the mummy talk over the telephone?
A: Because he was all tied up.

Months

Q: Will February March?
A: No, but April May.

❐

Did you hear about the guy who stole the judge's calendar?
He got 12 months.

❐

Gus: What is a liar's favorite month?
Gabriel: Who knows?
Gus: Fib-ruary.

Mosquitoes

Jeff: What is a mosquito's favorite sport?
Joel: My mind is blank.
Jeff: Skin diving.

☐

Christy: What's the happiest day in the life of a young mosquito?
Lisa: I'm in the dark.
Christy: The day it passes its screen test.

☐

Frustration: What happens when a mosquito bites a turnip.

☐

Edgar: How can you tell when there's a mosquito in your bed?
Emily: I don't know.
Edgar: By the M on its pajamas.

Mothers

Proud mother: Baby Ben is a year old now, and he's been walking since he was eight months old.

Bored listener: Really? He must be awfully tired.

☐

My mom's tough. Once when she said, "No," I said, "Jimmy's mother always lets him do it." I got sent to my room. Jimmy and his mother got sent to their rooms too.

☐

In a bakery window: Pie like mother used to buy.

☐

What ride makes mothers and babies scream?
A stroller coaster.

Moths

Peggy: How can you recognize a gypsy moth?
Paul: Beats me.
Peggy: It tries to tell your fortune.

❐

Geneva: What animal is satisfied with the least nourishment?
Guthrie: You tell me.
Geneva: Moths. They eat nothing but holes.

❐

Levi: Why doesn't the joker use mothballs to get rid of moths?
Lois: I don't know.
Levi: He can't aim those tiny mothballs to hit the moths.

❐

Calvin: Do moths cry?
Cora: That's a mystery.
Calvin: Yes. Haven't you ever seen a moth bawl?

❐

Leah: Where do moths dance?
Lawrence: I'm in the dark.
Leah: At a mothball.

❐

Why did the moth eat a hole in the rug?
Because it wanted to see the floor show.

Motorcycles

Nit: What do you get when you cross a motorcycle with a joke book?
Wit: That's a mystery.
Nit: A yamahaha.

❐

Clem: What do you call a cotton-eating insect that rides a motorcycle?
Slim: That's a mystery.
Clem: Weevil Knievel.

Mouths

Edgar: How do you glue your mouth shut?
Emily: My mind is blank.
Edgar: With lipstick.

❐

Levi: Why did the joker brush his teeth with gunpowder?
Lois: I have no clue.
Levi: He wanted to shoot his mouth off.

❐

Well, I wouldn't say that Mrs. Jones has a big mouth, but every time she smiles she gets lipstick on her ears.

❐

My loony secretary isn't an office gossip. She's a magician. She can turn an eyeful or an earful into a mouthful.

Movies

What is the most boring Clark Gable film?
Yawn with the Wind.

❐

Claud: What did the joker get when he crossed a swimming pool with a movie theater?
Chloe: I have no idea.
Claud: A dive-in movie.

❐

Bob: I'll have you know, I have royal blood in my veins.
Jim: Who's? King Kong's?

❐

A man threw a nickel toward the blind man's cup. The coin missed and rolled along the pavement, but the man with the dark glasses quickly recovered it.

"But I thought you were blind!"

"No, I am not the regular blind man, sir," he said, "I'm just taking his place while he's at the movies."

Music

Snoring: Sheet music.

❐

What did the musician say?
Nothing of note has been happening.

❐

Did you hear about the absentminded musician?
He had to leave himself notes.

❐

What did the pianist say?
Right on key.

❐

Bertram: What is a musician's favorite dessert?
Bernard: I can't guess.
Bertram: Cello.

❐

Lydia: What entertainment did Noah hire for the animals?
Larry: I give up.
Lydia: An ark-estra.

❐

How did the loony musician break his leg?
He fell over a clef.

❐

Christy: Did you get hurt when you fell and struck the piano?
Quentin: No, I hit the soft pedal.

❐

What did the drummer say?
It's hard to beat.

❐

Cecil: What has ten legs and sings?
Cyrus: Beats me.
Cecil: The Jackson Five.

❐

What do you call a singer who is not old enough to be a tenor?
A niner!

❐

Gertrude: Why did the teeny bopper hold a stone up to her left ear
and a hamburger bun up to her right ear?
Gerard: I have no clue.
Gertrude: Because she wanted to hear rock-and-roll.

❐

Gideon: What music do steelworkers play at their parties?
Gloria: My mind is a blank.
Gideon: Heavy metal.

❐

Stuffy singer: I sing with the voice of a bird.
Listener: I know—a crow.

❐

Leonard: What does the lighthouse keeper play in the village orchestra?
Leona: I can't guess.
Leonard: The foghorn.

❐

What does a tuba call his father?
Oompah-pah.

❐

Singer: Did you notice how my voice filled the whole room tonight?
Friend: Yes, a lot of people had to leave to make room for it.

❐

Edna: What color is a guitar?
Eldon: My mind's a blank.
Edna: Plink!

❐

Q: Why are jazz musicians sweet?
A: Because they play in jam sessions.

❐

Abner: What is hard to beat?
Agatha: I don't have the foggiest.
Abner: A drum with a hole in it.

❐

Edna: What kind of phone can make music?
Eldon: I have no idea.
Edna: A saxophone.

❐

Clem: What is a needy musician's fund called?
Slim: I give up.
Clem: A band-aid.

❐

Cornelius: What can you play on a shoehorn?
Henrietta: That's a mystery.
Cornelius: Sole music!

❐

Clem: What's an organ grinder's favorite tempo?
Slim: I'm blank.
Clem: Throw-quarter time!

N

Names

Jonas: I'll bet my name is harder than yours.
Jon-Mark: All right, what's your name?
Jonas: Stone.
Jon-Mark: You lose. My name is Harder.

◻

Abner: What do you call a man with a spade on his head?
Agatha: I can't guess.
Abner: Doug.

◻

Abner: What do you call a man without a spade on his head?
Agatha: I can't guess.
Abner: Douglas.

◻

Ambrose: What is the only thing you can break when you say its name?
Stella: You've got me.
Ambrose: Silence.

◻

Ambrose: What has never been felt, never been seen, never been heard, never existed, and still has a name?
Stella: You've got me guessing.
Ambrose: Nothing.

◻

What do you call a girl who is in charge of the woman's movement?
Libby.

◻

What do you call a guy who is a lookout for the Coast Guard?
Seymour.

◻

What do you call a guy who changes tires?
Jack.

❏

What do you call a guy who sleeps on a leaf pile?
Russell.

❏

Gustave: What belongs to you, but is used more often by others?
Gilberta: I don't have a clue.
Gustave: Your name.

❏

Lynette: What is another name people give their mistakes?
LeRoy: I pass.
Lynette: Experience.

❏

Laurel: What is the name for an older person who keeps your mother from spanking you?
LaVonne: I pass.
Laurel: A grandparent.

❏

Leah: What is another name for a nightclub?
Lawrence: I'm blank.
Leah: A rolling pin.

❏

What do you call a guy who can't light a firecracker?
Dudley.

❏

What is the wife of a jeweler called?
Ruby.

❏

What do you call a guy who fell ten floors from a building and landed on his head?
Spike.

❏

What do you call a girl who is very interested in Gypsies?
Crystal.

❒

Ferdinand: What do you call a man who lives on a back street?
Gertrude: It's unknown to me.
Ferdinand: Ali.

❒

Wilber: What do you call a man who likes throwing things?
Wanda: That's a mystery.
Wilber: Chuck.

❒

Wilber: What is that selfish girl's name?
Wanda: I don't know.
Wilber: Mimi.

National

What this country needs . . .
. . . a safety net for people who jump to conclusions.
. . . a transmission that will shift the blame.
. . . a song for unsung heroes.

Nature

Quentin: What is the difference between the rising and the setting sun?
Obadiah: I have no idea.
Quentin: All the difference in the world.

❒

Lila: What did one volcano say to the other volcano?
Lillian: Who knows?
Lila: I lava you.

❒

Fred: What did one earthquake say to the other earthquake?
Ted: You tell me.
Fred: It's all your fault.

❐

Arty: The tornado that blew my father's car away left another in its place.
Smarty: Must have been a trade wind.

❐

Quentin: What is the difference between a hill and a pill?
Obadiah: You tell me.
Quentin: One is hard to get up, while the other is hard to get down.

Needlework

Did you hear about the knitting needle that told jokes?
It could keep you in stitches.

❐

Rex: What did one needle say to another needle?
Tex: You tell me.
Rex: Sew tell me, what's new?

Noses

Carter: I broke my nose in two places.
Clara: You better stay out of those places.

❐

Q: No matter how smart you are, there is one thing you will always overlook. What is it?
A: Your nose.

❐

Derek: What smells most in a perfume shop?
Dorcus: Beats me.
Derek: Your nose.

❐

Q: Why is your nose not twelve inches long?
A: Because then it would be a foot.

Nursery Rhymes

Luther: If Mother Hubbard found a frankfurter for her dog, what kind of world would it be?
Lydia: I can't guess.
Luther: A dog-eat-dog world.

❐

What sign did the real estate agent put in front of the Old Woman Who Lived in a Shoe's house?
Soled.

❐

Carter: Who writes nursery rhymes and squeezes oranges?
Clara: I can't guess.
Carter: Mother Juice.

❐

Lisa: What did Humpty-Dumpty die of?
Lucile: I have no clue.
Lisa: Shell shock.

❐

Lydia: What did Mary order when she went out for dinner?
Larry: Who knows?
Lydia: Everybody knows that Mary had a little lamb.

❐

Who do mice see when they get sick?
The Hickory Dickory Doc.

❐

Ambrose: What did Humpty-Dumpty do after the fall?
Agatha: You tell me.
Ambrose: He called his lawyer.

Nuts

Fred: What would you get if you crossed a nut and a briefcase?
Ted: I have no idea.
Fred: A nut case.

❐

What do you call a nut that never remembers?
A forget-me-nut.

❐

Leah: What nut sounds like a sneeze?
Lawrence: It's unknown to me.
Leah: Cashew nut.

❐

Wilber: What is brown, hairy, and wears sunglasses?
Wanda: I give up.
Wilber: A coconut on vacation.

❐

Q: How do you know that peanuts are fattening?
A: Because you never see a skinny elephant.

❐

Cornelius: What kind of person loves cocoa?
Henrietta: You tell me.
Cornelius: A coconut.

Octopuses

Abner: What's red, white, and blue, and has lots of arms?
Agatha: Search me.
Abner: An octopus carrying an American flag.

Optometrists

Bill: Why did the optometrist and his wife have an argument?
Jill: I don't know.
Bill: They couldn't see eye to eye.

❐

"My business is looking better," said the loony optometrist.

❐

Q: Why is an eye doctor like a teacher?
A: They both test pupils.

P

Pants

Fred: What's the best kind of trousers for a wise guy to wear?
Ted: Who knows?
Fred: Smarty-pants.

❏

Geraldine: Why do golfers wear two pairs of pants?
Gaspar: I can't guess.
Geraldine: In case they get a hole in one.

❏

Leonard: If you reached into your pants pockets and pulled out a ten-dollar bill from each pocket, what would you have?
Leona: My mind's a blank.
Leonard: Somebody else's pants on.

❏

Q: Why are the boy's pants always too short?
A: Because feet are always sticking out.

❏

Tom: Your overalls are all wet.
Pete: I know, I just washed them.
Tom: Then why are you wearing them?
Pete: Because the label says: Wash and wear.

❏

Math teacher: Roderick, if I had ten quarters in my left pocket, ten dimes in my right, and ten nickels in both of my back pockets, what would I have?
Roderick: Heavy pants.

Parrots

Gustave: What squawks and jumps out of airplanes?
Gilberta: I don't have the foggiest.
Gustave: A parrot-trooper.

❏

Gwendolyn: What did the parrot say to the streetcar?
Godfrey: I don't have a clue.
Gwendolyn: Trolley want a cracker?

❏

Wilber: What do you get if you cross a centipede and a parrot?
Wanda: I'm in the dark.
Wilber: A walkie-talkie.

Peacocks

Fred: What do you get if you cross a peacock with an insect?
Ted: I give up.
Fred: A cocky roach.

❏

Cyrus: What sort of story did the peacock tell?
Cornelia: I can't guess.
Cyrus: A big tale.

Penguins

Claud: What's black and white and goes around and around?
Chloe: You've got me.
Claud: A penguin in a revolving door.

❏

Lana: What is black and white and black and white?
Lark: My mind is a blank.
Lana: A penguin tumbling down an iceberg.

❏

What is black and white and red on Christmas Eve?
Rudolph the Red-Nosed Penguin.

People

Q: When is a man not a man?
A: When he turns into an alley.

❐

Customer: This shop is a disgrace. I can write my name in the dust on this furniture.
Assistant: It must be wonderful to have an education.

❐

The problem with most parents today is that they give their kids a free hand . . . but not in the right place.

❐

Boss: Did your supervisor tell you what to do?
New employee: Yes, sir. He told me to wake him up if I saw you coming.

❐

Q: When is a boy not a boy?
A: When he's a little hoarse.

Pet Stores

My business is for the birds, said the loony pet store owner.

❐

Q: Have you heard of the new pet shop in Greenwich Village?
A: Yes, it's called "Fish and Cheeps."

Pigs

Is Ballpoint really the name of your pig?
No, that's just his pen name.

❐

Where was deviled ham mentioned in the Bible?
When the evil spirits entered the swine.

❐

When is it proper to refer to a person as a pig?
When he is a boar.

❐

Show me a swine, and I'll show you hogwash.

❐

Cyrus: What animal is a tattletale?
Cornelia: I give up.
Cyrus: The pig always squeals on you.

❐

Debby: Is it true that pigs make good drivers?
Denise: I here that they're road hogs.

❐

What pen is never used for writing?
A pigpen.

❐

Q: Why are talkative people and male pigs alike?
A: Because after awhile both of them become bores (boars).

❐

Q: Why shouldn't you tell a pig a secret?
A: Because he's a squealer.

❐

What rolls in the mud and plays trick-or-treat?
The Halloween Pig.

❐

Lois: Where does a pig go to pawn his watch?
Lola: I'm in the dark.
Lois: He goes to a ham hock shop.

❐

Allan: Tom was arrested for stealing a pig.
Dick: How did they prove it?
Allan: The pig squealed.

❐

Loony visitor: Why does that old hog keep trying to come into my room? Is it because he likes me?
Loony farmer: Not really, friend. You see, that's his room during the winter.

❐

Q: How does a pig get to the hospital?
A: In a hambulance!

❐

Farmer: How do you treat a pig with a sore throat?
Veterinarian: Apply oinkment.

❐

Clem: What is a sure way to grow fat?
Slim: How should I know?
Clem: Raise hogs.

❐

Leonard: Why did the three little pigs decide to leave home?
Leona: That's a mystery.
Leonard: They thought their father was an awful boar.

❐

Rob: Where do they keep all the pigs in Oregon?
Rachel: You've got me.
Rob: In the state pen.

❐

Abner: What did Farmer Jake get when he crossed a pig with a Christmas tree?
Agatha: I have no idea.
Abner: A porky pine.

❐

Q: Why did the farmer name his pig Ink?
A: Because it kept running out of the pen.

❐

Q: Why are hogs like trees?
A: Because they root for a living.

❐

Quentin: What do you call high-rise apartment houses for pigs?
Obadiah: I have no clue.
Quentin: Skyscrapers.

Pizza

We just heard that Italy is sponsoring a new award for excellence in the art of cooking pizza. It's called the Nobel Pizza Prize.

❐

Rudolph: What is a piece of Italian pie?
Thelma: I'm in the dark.
Rudolph: A pizza pie.

Plants

Lisa: How did one cactus compliment another cactus?
Lucile: I have no idea.
Lisa: You look sharp today.

Plumbers

Arnold: Why was the plumber so tired?
Amy: You tell me.
Arnold: He felt drained.

❐

Ambrose: What does it take to be a plumber?
Agatha: You've got me.
Ambrose: Pipe dreams.

❐

What is a diploma?
Da man who fixa da pipes when dey leak.

◻

My neck's as stiff as a pipe, my head's like a lump of lead and my nose is all stopped up. I don't need a doctor—I need a plumber.

◻

What does the plumber say to his wife when she talks too much?
Pipe down.

◻

If a gardener has a green thumb, who has a purple thumb?
A nearsighted plumber.

Police

Edgar: How did the police describe the hitchhiker?
Emily: Beats me.
Edgar: They gave a thumbnail description.

◻

Bertram: What did the police say when a famous drawing was stolen?
Bernard: You tell me.
Bertram: Details are sketchy.

◻

Did you hear about the shoplifter at the lingerie shop?
She gave police the slip.

◻

Claud: What do you call a man who bites a policeman?
Chloe: I'm a blank.
Claud: A law a-biting citizen.

◻

If dentists pull out police officers' teeth, what do police do to dentists' teeth?
Pull them over.

◻

I live in a high-crime neighborhood. Even our police station has a burglar alarm.

Politics

Rusty: If the head of the United States is called the President and the head of England is the Prime Minister, what is the head of Nova Scotia called?
Dusty: I don't know. What?
Rusty: The Bossa Nova.

❐

Bill: Why isn't the elderly female mayor getting reelected?
Jill: You tell me.
Bill: Because the old gray mayor ain't what she used to be.

❐

The trouble with dark-horse candidates is you can't find out about their track record until you are saddled with them.

❐

Griff: My Uncle Guy is running for mayor.
Gretta: Honest?
Griff: No, but that's not stopping him.

❐

Joe: Here's one name on the committee that I've never heard of.
Moe: Oh, that's probably the person who actually does the work.

❐

Doreen: Why does it take so long to make a politician snowman?
Duncan: You tell me.
Doreen: You have to hollow out the head first.

Porcupines

Abner: How do you move in a crowd of porcupines?
Abigail: My mind is a blank.
Abner: Very carefully.

❐

Cecil: What did the near-sighted porcupine say when it backed into a cactus?
Cyrus: That's a mystery.
Cecil: Pardon me, honey.

❐

Nit: What do you get if you cross a porcupine with a peacock?
Wit: My mind is blank.
Nit: A sharp dresser.

❐

Cyrus: What would you get if you crossed a porcupine and a skunk?
Cornelia: I'm a blank.
Cyrus: A smelly pincushion.

Potatoes

Lola: Where was the first french fry made?
Lionel: Search me.
Lola: In Greece.

❐

Cyrus: What do you get if you cross a potato with an onion?
Cornelia: You tell me.
Cyrus: A potato with watery eyes.

❐

Q: Why do some monkeys sell potato chips?
A: Because they're chip monks.

❐

Rex: What do you get if you cross a potato with a beet?
Tex: You've got me.
Rex: A potato with bloodshot eyes.

❐

Art: What did the baked potato say to the cook?
Bart: You tell me.
Art: Foiled again!

❐

Kermit: What has eyes but can't see?
Zackery: You tell me.
Kermit: A potato.

Professions

Barnaby: Why was the lifeguard at the store?
Barbie: I can't guess.
Barnaby: He heard he could save a lot.

❏

What did the gunsmith say?
Booming!

❏

What did the locksmith say?
Everything's opening up.

❏

Did you hear about the sword swallower who worked for nothing?
He was a free-lancer.

❏

Bill: Want to know why I stopped going to the masseur?
Jill: Sure, tell me.
Bill: He rubbed me the wrong way.

❏

Geraldine: What do magicians say on Halloween?
Gaspar: Tell me.
Geraldine: Trick or treat.

❏

Falsehood: Someone who pretends to be a gangster.

❏

Gideon: What do you call the boss at a dairy?
Gloria: Who knows?
Gideon: The big cheese.

❏

What did the botanist say?
Everything's coming up roses.

❐

What did the floor waxer say?
Going smoothly.

❐

Did you hear the story about the snake trainers? It was rather charming.

❐

You tell 'em, hunter. I'm game.

❐

What kind of goofy waiter never accepts tips?
A dumb waiter.

❐

Who was the greatest Irish inventor?
Pat Pending.

❐

You tell 'cm, operator. You've got their number.

❐

Garth: I'm going to have to let that new secretary go.
Gertha: Don't you think he is learning word processing fast enough?
Garth: I don't think so. There is too much White-Out on the monitor screen!

❐

What did the counterfeiter say?
We're forging on.

❐

What did the counterman say?
Pretty crummy.

❐

Laurel: Why are loony writers the strangest creatures in the world?
LaVonne: How should I know?
Laurel: Because their tales come out of their heads.

❏

Fox: Who dares to sit before the queen with his hat on?
Owl: Her chauffeur.

❏

Leah: How do you become a coroner?
Lawrence: I don't know.
Leah: You have to take a stiff examination.

❏

What did the demolition worker say?
Smashing!

❏

What did the street cleaner say?
Things are picking up.

❏

Sign in a Loonyville flower shop: Love 'em and leaf 'em.

❏

A Loonyville movie star returned to his boyhood home for the first time since he became famous.

"I guess everyone around here talks a lot about me," the star said to the Loonyville mayor.

"That's right," agreed the Loonyville mayor. "You're so famous we even put a sign in front of your old house."

The Loonyville movie star beamed. "Really?" he exclaimed. "What does the sign say?"

Smiling broadly, the Loonyville mayor replied, "It says, 'Stop'!"

❏

Loony Leroy: Did you hear about the poet who got arrested for writing too fast?
Loony Lester: No, what about him?
Loony Leroy: The judge took away his poetic license.

❏

"My business is sick," said the loony doctor.

❐

"My business is going up," said the loony elevator operator.

❐

Did you hear about the loony student who got a real shock? He thought electricians' school was going to be easy.

❐

A business executive decided to ask a few friends the question, "How's business?" Their answers:
Astronomer: Looking up.
Author: Mine seems to be all write.
Butcher: We're making ends meat.
Tobacconist: Going up in smoke.
Exterminator: We're gradually getting the bugs out.

❐

What did the gravedigger say?
Monumental!

❐

What did the photographer say?
Everything is clicking and developing well.

❐

Q: Where does a soda jerk learn his trade?
A: In sundae school.

❐

Abner: What would you call a man who is always wiring for money?
Agatha: That's a mystery.
Abner: An electrician.

❐

Q: When does a public speaker steal lumber?
A: When he takes the floor.

❐

Q: Why was the photographer arrested?
A: Because he shot people and blew them up.

❐

Q: Why is a thief like a thermometer on a hot day?
A: Because they are both up to something.

❐

Ryan: What can you tell me of the great chemists of the seventeenth century?
Mark: I have no clue.
Ryan: They are all dead.

❐

Waiter: A man who believes money grows on trays.

❐

Shopper: Someone who likes to go buy-buy.

❐

Q: How did the man describe his work in the towel factory?
A: Very absorbing.

❐

Edna: What shoemaker makes shoes without any leather?
Eldon: I can't guess.
Edna: A blacksmith makes horseshoes.

❐

Q: When are cooks most cruel?
A: When they beat the eggs and whip the cream.

❐

Husband (shakily as he brings home flowers for his wife): The florist was held up by an armed robber. You might describe the man as a pet-rified florist.

❐

Kermit: What did the judge say when a skunk walked into the court-room?

Zackery: I give up.
Kermit: Odor in the court!

❒

Car dealer: This car has had just one careful owner.
Buyer: But look at it—it's a wreck.
Car dealer: The other five owners weren't so careful, I have to admit.

Psychiatrists

Jon-Mark: Imagine meeting you here at the psychiatrist's office! Are you coming or going?
Jonas: If I knew that, I wouldn't be here!

❒

Patient: Help me, Doc. I keep making long distance calls to myself and I'm going broke!
Psychiatrist: Try reversing the charges.

❒

Psychiatrist: Well, George, you're making great progress, which is more than I can say for Stanley in Ward J. He keeps telling everyone he's going to buy the Vatican! Can you believe that?
George: No, I can't. After all, I've told him a million times I won't sell.

❒

Patient: Doctor, my life is a mess. I just don't think I can go on this way anymore.
Psychiatrist: Yes, we all have problems. I can help you, but it'll take time. We'll start at four sessions a week. My fee is a hundred dollars an hour.
Patient: Well, that solves your problem. What about mine?

R

Rabbits

How did the barber get rid of his unwanted rabbits?
He used hare remover.

Fred: What do you call a contented rabbit?
Ted: You've got me.
Fred: Hoppy-go-lucky.

Cecil: What do you call a rabbit that has never been out of the house?
Cyrus: I'm blank.
Cecil: An ingrown hare.

Pam: How do you paint a rabbit?
Melba: That's a mystery.
Pam: With hare spray.

Lola: Which rabbit stole from the rich to give to the poor?
Lionel: I can't guess.
Lola: Rabbit Hood.

Bertram: What do you call 300 rabbits marching backward?
Bernard: I have no clue.
Bertram: A receding hareline.

Q: How can you find a lost rabbit?
A: Make a noise like a carrot.

Gaylord: What would you get if you blew your hair dryer down a rabbit hole?
Gladys: My mind is a blank.
Gaylord: Hot, cross bunnies.

❐

What did the rabbits do after they got married?
Went on their bunnymoon.

❐

Abner: What is the difference between a crazy hare and a counterfeit coin?
Agatha: Who knows?
Abner: One is a mad bunny, and the other is bad money.

❐

Peggy: How do you catch a unique bunny?
Paul: Who knows?
Peggy: Unique up on him.

❐

Peggy: How do you catch a tame bunny?
Paul: You've got me.
Peggy: The tame way.

❐

Wilber: What do you call a rabbit that likes to swim with alligators?
Wanda: I pass.
Wilber: Dinner.

❐

What is a rabbit's favorite song?
Hoppy Birthday.

❐

Abner: What do you get from petting rabbits with sharp teeth?
Agatha: I give up.
Abner: Hare cuts.

Reptiles

What would you get if you crossed an alligator with a pickle?
A crocodill.

☐

Geraldine: What kind of lizard loves riddles?
Gaspar: I don't have the foggiest.
Geraldine: A sillymander.

☐

Gustave: What changes color every two seconds?
Gilberta: I give up.
Gustave: A chameleon with the hiccups.

Rhinoceros

What do you get if you cross a rhinoceros and a goose?
An animal that honks before it runs you over.

☐

Geneva: What has one eye, one horn, and flies?
Guthrie: Who knows?
Geneva: A half-blind rhinoceros in an airplane.

☐

Abner: How did the joker fit a rhinoceros into his car?
Abigail: You've got me.
Abner: He made one of the elephants get out.

Rooms

Calvin: If a man was locked up in a room with only a bat and a piano, how could he get out?
Cora: You tell me.

Calvin: There are two ways: He could swing the bat three times for an out, or use a piano key.

❏

Laurel: Which is the largest room in the world?
LaVonne: Beats me.
Laurel: The room for improvement.

❏

Leah: What room can no one enter?
Lawrence: I have no clue.
Leah: A mushroom.

❏

Luther: What happens when 500 people rush to get accommodations in a hotel that has only 400 rooms?
Lydia: Beats me.
Luther: They race for space.

❏

I was going to straighten my room yesterday, but I couldn't find the rake and shovel.

❏

Ryan: What room do you bounce around in?
Mark: How should I know?
Ryan: A ballroom.

❏

Mom says my room looks like a cyclone hit it, but that's not true. If a cyclone hit it, it would be neater.

S

Sailors

Q: When does the captain of a yacht get a traffic ticket for careless piloting?
A: When he sails past a red lighthouse.

❐

Fox: Who is the smallest man in history?
Owl: The sailor who went to sleep on his watch.

❐

What did the sailor say?
Knot bad.

❐

Q: When is a sailor not a sailor?
A: When he's aboard.

❐

Cecil: What did the first shipwrecked sailor say when the second sailor was washed ashore?
Cyrus: How should I know?
Cecil: Now we have two on the isle.

Salesmen

Bertram: What do you call a tire salesman?
Bernard: Beats me.
Bertram: A wheeler-dealer.

❐

Edna: What does a real estate salesman have to know?
Eldon: Beats me.
Edna: Lots.

❐

First salesman: My job is selling salt.
Second Salesman: Why, that's my job, too!
First salesman: Shake.

Santa Claus

Rob: Where does Saint Nick go on holidays?
Rachel: Who knows?
Rob: On a Santa Cruz.

❏

Show me Santa's helpers, and I'll show you subordinate clauses.

❏

Geneva: Who rides in a sleigh, gives Christmas presents, and has many faults?
Guthrie: Beats me.
Geneva: Santa Flaws.

❏

A man goes through three stages:
He believes in Santa,
He doesn't believe in Santa,
He is Santa!

❏

Sign in big store: "Five Santas, No Waiting."

❏

Rudolph: What is a clumsy Santa Claus?
Thelma: How should I know?
Rudolph: A Santa Klutz.

❏

Where does Santa stay overnight when he travels?
At ho-ho-hotels.

❏

Claustrophobia: Fear of Santa.

❐

Calvin: What is the name of the person who brings gifts to the dentist's office?
Cora: I have no clue.
Calvin: Santa Floss.

❐

Fox: Who has a sack and bites people?
Owl: Santa Jaws.

❐

Fox: Who is Santa Claus's wife?
Owl: Mary Christmas.

School

Teacher: When was the Great Depression?
Student: Last week when I got my report card.

❐

Did you hear about the kid who was 20 minutes early for school?
He was in a class by himself.

❐

Did you hear about the successful school play?
It was a class act.

❐

Arnold: Why did the class clown give a smart girl a dog biscuit?
Amy: I can't guess.
Arnold: He heard she was the teacher's pet.

❐

Arnold: Why are you shivering, Amy?
Amy: I guess it must be this zero on my test paper.

❐

Gaylord: Why do thermometers go to school?
Gladys: I can't guess.
Gaylord: To earn their degrees.

❒

First teacher: Gene got a zero on the test today.
Second teacher: That's nothing.

❒

Teacher: Donald, can you give me one use for a horsehide?
Donald: Well, I guess it helps to hold the horse together.

❒

Why is a schoolyard larger at recess?
Because there are more feet in it.

❒

Gaylord: What is big and yellow and comes in the morning to brighten mother's day?
Gladys: Who knows?
Gaylord: The school bus.

❒

One goofy kid in our class dresses terribly. The only thing that matches on him is his belt size and his IQ.

❒

First student: The teacher gave me an F-minus.
Second student: Why did she do that?
First student: She says I not only didn't learn anything this year, but I probably forgot most of the stuff I learned last year as well.

❒

Endangered species: A kid who gets straight F's on his report card.

❒

We have a kid in our class who dresses like a million bucks. Everything he wears is wrinkled and green.

❒

Geraldine: What does a student need if he is absent from school during the final exams?
Gaspar: You tell me.
Geraldine: A good excuse.

❐

A little boy showed his teacher his drawing, entitled "America the Beautiful." In the center was an airplane covered with apples, pears, oranges, and bananas.
"What is this?" the teacher asked, pointing to the airplane.
"That," answered the boy, "is the fruited plane."

❐

The meat at lunch today was so tough that half the class was kept after school so we could finish chewing it.

❐

Lynette: What do you call it when your teacher phones your parents to tell them how poorly you're doing in school?
LeRoy: I don't know.
Lynette: A bad connection.

❐

Loony student: Teacher, is there life after death?
Teacher: Why do you ask?
Loony student: I may need the extra time to finish all this homework you gave us.

❐

Teacher: Everyone knows we should conserve energy. Larry, name one way we can do that.
Loony Larry: By staying in bed all day.

❐

Teacher: When did George Washington die?
Loony Lester: It was just a few days before they buried him.

❐

Teacher: Leena, what is the first thing you should do with a barrel of crude oil?
Loony Leena: Teach it some manners.

❐

Teacher: Why should we never use the word "ain't"?
Loony Leroy: Because it ain't correct.

❐

What school do toothbrushes go to?
Colgate.

❐

Nick: First I got tonsillitis, followed by appendicitis and pneumonia, ending up with neuritis. Then they gave me hypodermics and inoculations.
Rick: Boy, did you have a hard time!
Nick: I'll say. I thought I'd never pull through that spelling test.

❐

Did you hear about the loony speech school? They teach you how to speak clearly. To do this they fill your mouth with marbles. You are supposed to talk clearly right through the marbles. Every day you lose one marble. When you've lost all your marbles . . . you're done.

❐

What is harder than cutting school?
Gluing it back together.

❐

I don't know why it's so important to finish your homework. As soon as you get it done, they just give you more.

❐

Principal: Now, Amanda, did you really call your teacher a meany?
Amanda: Yes, I did.
Principal: And is it true you called her a wicked old witch?
Amanda: Yes, it is.

Principal: And did you call her a tomato-nosed beanbag?
Amanda: No, but I'll remember that one for next time!

❐

Teacher: We are only going to have half a day's lessons this morning.
Pupils: Hurrah!
Teacher: Yes, we will be having the other half this afternoon.

❐

One kid in our class has never missed or been late with one single homework assignment. The rest of the class was so proud of him that we chipped in and bought him a television set.

❐

Sammy had just completed his first day at school.
Mother: Well, what did you learn today?
Sammy: Not enough. I have to go back tomorrow.

❐

Teacher: Give me a sentence with an object.
Student: You're very beautiful, teacher.
Teacher: What is the object?
Student: A good grade.

❐

Sign at a community college: "If Your Mind Isn't Becoming You, You Should Be Coming Here."

Seals

Barnaby: Why did the seal cross the road?
Barbie: You've got me.
Barnaby: To get to the otter side.

❐

Abner: What kind of seal does housework?
Agatha: It's unknown to me.
Abner: The Good Housekeeping Seal.

Sheep

Ferdinand: What do you get if a sheep studies karate?
Gertrude: I'm blank.
Ferdinand: A lamb chop.

❐

Luann: Which eats more grass—black sheep or white?
Lowell: I'm blank.
Luann: White, because there are more of them.

❐

Wilma: What's a sheep's favorite snack?
Wesley: You've got me.
Wilma: A baa-loney sandwich.

❐

Levi: Why did the farmer feed his sheep chunks of steel?
Lois: You've got me.
Levi: He wanted them to grow steel wool.

❐

Where do sheep go when they want to barter?
To the five-and-ten because they know they will get their Woolworth.

❐

Derek: What animal disbelieves everything?
Dorcus: You've got me guessing.
Derek: Sheep. They always say, "Bah, bah!"

❐

Q: Why are sheep poor?
A: Because they're always getting fleeced.

❐

Modern Mary
Mary had a little lamb
Given her to keep.
It followed her around until
It died from lack of sleep.

❐

Ryan: What do you call the place where they shear sheep?
Mark: I have no idea.
Ryan: A baa-baa shop.

Shoes

Q: Why can't a shoe talk?
A: Because it's tongue-tied.

◻

Gertrude: What shoes should you wear when your basement is flooded?
Gerard: Who knows?
Gertrude: Pumps.

◻

I had one friend who was a real dummy. He lost his shoes one time because he put them on the wrong feet. Then he couldn't remember whose feet he put them on.

◻

Then there was the goofy man who put on one boot because the weather forecaster said there would be only one foot of snow.

◻

If you threw a green shoe into the Red Sea, what would it become?
Wet.

◻

Cecil: What kind of problem does a five-foot man have?
Cyrus: It's unknown to me.
Cecil: He needs two-and-a-half pairs of shoes!

◻

Did you ever see a shoe box?

◻

Ferdinand: What wears shoes but has no feet?
Gertrude: I don't have the foggiest.
Ferdinand: The pavement.

Singing

Kermit: What is it that everyone has to catch before he can sing?
Zackery: Who knows?
Kermit: His breath.

Sinks

Eileen: How do you make a kitchen sink?
Olivia: Beats me.
Eileen: Throw it in the ocean.

❐

Levi: Why did Santa have only seven reindeer on Christmas Eve?
Lois: I'm in the dark.
Levi: Comet was home cleaning the sink.

❐

What piece of furniture will never learn to swim?
The sink.

Sisters

First boy: What's the best way to teach a girl to swim?
Second boy: That requires technique. First, you put your left arm around her waist. Then you gently take her left hand and—
First boy: She's my sister.
Second boy: Oh! Then you just push her off the dock!

❐

What is the difference between kissing your sister and kissing your sweetheart?
About 25 seconds.

❐

Alfred: Grandpa, what do I have to know to teach my sister Clara tricks?
Grandpa: More than Clara.

Size

Gruesome: A little taller than before.

◻

Who is the smallest man mentioned in the Bible?
Some people believe that it was Zacchaeus. Others believe it was Nehemiah (Knee-high-a-miah), or Bildad, the Shuhite (Shoe-height). But in reality it was Peter the disciple. He slept on his watch.

◻

Which burns longer: a white candle or a black one?
Neither. Both burn shorter.

◻

How long is a Chinaman?
Of course! (How Long is his name.)

◻

Did you ever hear of Amoebae State Prison? It's so small it has only one cell.

◻

Eileen: How much sand would be in a hole one foot long, one foot wide, and one foot deep?
Olivia: You've got me.
Eileen: None, silly. There is no sand in a hole.

◻

What does 36 inches make in Glasgow?
One Scotland Yard.

◻

Geraldine: What amusement-park ride is only 12 inches long?
Gaspar: I don't know.
Geraldine: A ruler coaster.

◻

Why was the loony woman always able to remember the names of people under five feet tall?
Because she had a short memory.

❐

Q: Why shouldn't you have a short walking stick?
A: Because it would never be-long to you.

❐

The loony boy was so big that he could only play seek.

❐

That guy is so frail and skinny that the last time someone kicked sand in his face, the grains knocked him out cold.

❐

Q: Why should the number 288 never be mentioned in polite company?
A: Because it is two gross (too gross).

Skeletons

Two skeletons went to a dance. The first skeleton said to the second skeleton, "Why aren't you dancing?"
"I've got no body to dance with," the second skeleton replied.

❐

Edgar: How do you make a skeleton laugh?
Emily: You've got me.
Edgar: Tickle its funny bone.

❐

Q: If you lived in a graveyard, what would you open the gate with?
A: A skeleton key.

Skirts

Show me a girl who shuns the miniskirt, and I'll show you a hemlock.

❐

Grover: What does Mickey Mouse's girlfriend wear?
Gretchen: That's a mystery.
Grover: Minnie skirts.

Skunks

What is the difference between an excited skunk and a calm skunk?
An $80 laundry bill.

❐

Derek: What is the best way to talk to a skunk?
Dorcus: My mind's a blank.
Derek: By long distance.

❐

Grover: What do you get when you cross a skunk with a raccoon?
Gretchen: I don't have the foggiest.
Grover: A dirty look from the raccoon.

❐

Lola: Where does a skunk sit in church?
Lionel: I have no idea.
Lola: In a pew.

❐

Ichabod: If a skunk got its nose cut off, how would it smell?
Eutychus: I don't know.
Ichabod: As bad as ever.

❐

What is the skunk's motto?
Walk softly and carry a big stink.

❐

Q: How many skunks does it take to smell up the neighborhood?
A: Just a phew.

❐

Cornelius: What is a midget skunk called?
Henrietta: I'm blank.
Cornelius: A shrunk skunk.

Sleep

Levi: Why does the joker go to bed with 50 cents every night?
Lois: I pass.
Levi: They're his sleeping quarters.

❏

Cyrus: What should you do if you find a gorilla asleep in your bed?
Cornelia: I have no clue.
Cyrus: Sleep somewhere else.

❏

One of the first things Cain did after he left the Garden of Eden was to take a nap. How do we know this?
Because he went to the land of Nod—Genesis 4:16.

❏

Rufus: What did the mama broom and the papa broom say to the baby broom?
Rachel: I don't know.
Rufus: Go to sweep.

❏

Why is a sleeping baby like a hijacking?
Because it's a kid napping.

❏

Loony Lupie: Why is Daddy singing so much tonight?
Loony mother: He's trying to sing the baby to sleep before the baby-sitter gets here.
Loony Lupie: You know, if I were the baby, I'd pretend I was asleep.

❏

Wilber: What is a sleeping child?
Wanda: I have no idea.
Wilber: A kidnapper.

❏

Patient: Doctor, you've gotta do something for me. I snore so loudly that I wake myself up.
Loony doctor: In that case, sleep in another room.

❏

When did Moses sleep with five people in one bed?
When he slept with his forefathers.

❏

What do you call a guy who falls asleep on your front porch?
Matt.

❏

Eileen: How do you get rid of bedbugs?
Olivia: I have no clue.
Eileen: Make them sleep on the couch.

❏

Knapsack: A sleeping bag.

❏

Guy: Every morning I dream I'm falling from a 10-story building and just before I hit the ground, I wake up.
Grace: That's terrible. What are you going to do about it?
Guy: I'm going to move into a 15-story building. I need more sleep.

❏

Geoffe: Did you know there was a kidnapping down the street?
Geaney: No, what happened?
Geoffe: His mother woke him up.

❏

Laurel: What question can never be answered by saying yes?
LaVonne: Beats me.
Laurel: Are you asleep?

❏

Boss: Why are you so late?
Worker: I overslept.
Boss: You mean you sleep at home too?

❏

Q: Where does the sandman keep his sleeping bag?
A: In a nap sack.

❏

Jack: I haven't had any sleep for nine days.
Mack: That's terrible!
Jack: Fortunately, I don't have any trouble sleeping nights.

❏

What should you do when your sister falls asleep in church?
Polka.

❏

Meg: Why does your brother sleep in the chandelier?
Greg: Because he's a light sleeper.

Snails

Lisa: What restaurants do slow-moving snails avoid?
Lucile: That's a mystery.
Lisa: Fast-food places.

Snakes

What snake builds things?
A boa constructor.

❏

Q: Why is it so hard to fool a snake?
A: You can't pull his leg.

❏

What does a baby snake play with?
A rattle.

Socks

Gerald: I just love the holiday season!
Jack: Yeah, I always get a little sentimental about Christmas. In fact, every Christmas Eve I take off my socks and stand them in front of the fireplace.

□

Cornelius: What should I wear with yellow, green, and purple socks?
Henrietta: My mind's a blank.
Cornelius: Hip boots!

□

Q: What did Grandma do when she received a letter from her grandson saying he had grown another foot since she had last seen him?
A: She knitted another sock.

□

Lydia: What did the sock say to the needle?
Larry: I don't know.
Lydia: I'll be darned!

Sons

What man in the Bible had no parents?
Joshua, the son of Nun.

□

Loony son: I'm really glad you named me Larry.
Loony mother: Why?
Loony son: That's what the kids at school call me.

□

Q: Why did Mr. and Mrs. Newbert hire a tutor for their son?
A: So he could pass recess.

❑

Teacher: Mrs. Grey, your son is a constant troublemaker. How do you put up with him?
Mrs. Grey: I can't. That's why I sent him to school.

❑

Bertram: What did the barber call his son?
Bernard: Who knows?
Bertram: A little shaver.

❑

Which one of Noah's sons was considered to be a clown?
His second son. He was always a Ham.

❑

Father: My boy, when you grow up I want you to be a gentleman.
Son: I don't want to be a gentleman, Pop. I wanna be like you.

Soup

Doreen: Why is noodle soup good for you?
Duncan: I can't guess.
Doreen: Because it's brain food.

❑

Diner: What's your soup like today?
Waiter: Just like it was yesterday—only a day older.

❑

Diner: Waiter, I'm still waiting for the turtle soup I ordered.
Waiter: Well, sir, you know how slow turtles are.

❑

This one restaurant we went to used to make soup that was so greasy, if you sprinkled salt and pepper on it, they slid right off.

❑

They advertise a soup that will put color back into your cheeks. They don't tell you that the color is green.

❐

Diner: Waiter, there's a fly in my soup!
Loony waiter: Don't worry. The frog should snap it up any second now.

Spelling Bee

How do you spell Mississippi with one eye?
Close one eye and spell it.

❐

Q: If I was in the sun and you were out of it, what would the sun become?
A: Sin.

❐

How do you spell pickle backward?
P-I-C-K-L-E B-A-C-K-W-A-R-D.

❐

What occurs one in a minute, twice in a moment, but not once in a hundred years?
The letter M.

❐

Willard: What question do you always have to answer by saying Yes?
Wallace: I have no clue.
Willard: What does y-e-s spell?

❐

Q: Why is the letter K like a pig's tail?
A: Because it's the end of pork.

❐

Lynette: How many peas in a pint?
LeRoy: I don't know.
Lynette: One.

❐

Q: Why is an island like the letter T?
A: Because it is in the middle of water.

❐

Matthew and Mark have something that is not found in Luke and John. What is it?
The letter A.

❐

Christy: Mississippi is a very long word, but I can spell it.
Quentin: Okay, spell it.
Christy: I-T.

❐

Wilma: What starts with E and ends with E and has one letter in it?
Wesley: I have no idea.
Wilma: An envelope.

❐

Q: Can you spell "blind pig" with two letters?
A: Pg (pig without an eye.)

❐

Ryan: What letter should you avoid?
Mark: I don't know.
Ryan: The letter A because it makes men mean.

❐

Q: Why is the letter E like London?
A: Because it is the capital in England.

❐

Abner: What is the difference between here and there?
Agatha: You've got me.
Abner: The letter T.

❐

Q: When you take away two letters from this five-letter word, you are left with one. What's the word?
A: Stone.

❐

Wilber: What's the easiest way to widen a road?
Wanda: You've got me.
Wilber: Just add a B and it becomes broad right away.

❐

Ike: How do you make notes of stone?
Mike: I don't know.
Ike: Just rearrange the letters.

❐

Q: Why is the letter D like a bad boy?
A: Because it makes ma mad.

Spiders

Why are spiders good baseball players?
Because they know how to catch flies.

❐

Q: Why are spiders like tops?
A: They are always spinning.

Sports

When is a basketball player like a baby?
When he dribbles.

❐

Man: How many slopes did they have at the ski resort you went to?
Woman: Three . . . beginners, intermediate, and call-an-ambulance!

❐

Gustave: What does the sneezing champion of the Olympics win?
Gilberta: You've got me.
Gustave: A cold medal.

❐

Laurel: What do they call a boxer who gets beat up in a fight?
LaVonne: I have no clue.
Laurel: A sore loser.

❐

Loony mountain climber: Someone who wants to take a peak.

❐

Q: Where is the fencing master?
A: He's out to lunge.

❐

Ferdinand: What does the winner of the race lose?
Gertrude: I pass.
Ferdinand: His breath.

❐

Kermit: What is the difference between a skilled marksman and the man who tends the targets?
Zackery: I can't guess.
Kermit: One hits the mark, and the other marks the hits.

❐

Edna: What is the difference between the world's heavyweight boxing champion and a man with a cold?
Eldon: I don't know.
Edna: One knows his blows and the other blows his nose.

❐

Did you ever see a picket fence?

❐

Ryan: What is the quietest sport?
Mark: I don't know.
Ryan: Bowling. You can hear a pin drop.

Squirrels

Show me a squirrel's nest, and I'll show you the Nutcracker Suite.

❐

Cecil: What's the best way to catch a squirrel?
Cyrus: I have no idea.
Cecil: Climb a tree and act like a nut.

Stones

Bill: Why did the nutty kid put his head on the grindstone?
Jill: I give up.
Bill: To sharpen his wits.

❐

My loony boss has a heart of stone. He can even trace his roots back to a petrified forest.

❐

Derek: What does a stone become when it is in the water?
Dorcus: I can't guess.
Derek: A whetstone.

❐

Ferdinand: What's red and eats rocks?
Gertrude: I have no idea.
Ferdinand: A big red rock eater.

Storks

Edna: What bird can lift the heaviest weight?
Eldon: You've got me guessing.
Edna: A crane.

❐

Lila: Why is the stork associated with birth?
Lillian: I don't know.
Lila: Because we all come into this world stork naked.

❐

Stork: The bird with the big bill.

Strawberries

Eileen: How do you make a strawberry shake?
Olivia: I have no idea.
Eileen: Sneak up on it and say, "Boo!"

❐

What do you have when 134 strawberries try to get through the same door?
A strawberry jam.

Success

Ambrose: What's the Secret of Success?
Stella: It's unknown to me.
Ambrose: "Takes pain," said the window.
"Keep cool," said the ice.
"Drive hard," said the hammer.
"Be up to date," said the calendar.
"Never be led," said the pencil.
"Be sharp," said the knife.
"Make light around you," said the fire.
"Stick to it," said the glue.
"Be bright," said the lamp.

Summer Camp

Summer camp is educational. Last year I learned how to say "Help" underwater.

❐

Nit: Did you hear about the camper who swallowed the flashlight?
Wit: That's awful.
Nit: Yeah, he hiccuped with de-light.

Suspenders

Geneva: Why does Uncle Sam wear red, white, and blue suspenders?
Guthrie: I have no idea.
Geneva: To hold up his pants.

❐

Why is a bank robbery like a pair of suspenders?
Because they are both holdups.

❐

Leonard: What is the oldest form of social security?
Leona: You tell me.
Leonard: Suspenders.

❐

Aunt Bessie was so skinny she wore suspenders to hold up her girdle.

Swimming

Barnaby: Why is it never good to swim on an empty stomach?
Barbie: I have no idea.
Barnaby: Because it's easier to swim in water.

❐

My father taught me how to swim when I was five years old. He took me down to the river and threw me in. I wouldn't have minded, but people were ice skating at the time.

❐

Gideon: Why did the swimmer get a ticket?
Gloria: I have no idea.
Gideon: He was caught diving without a license.

❐

Gene: Did you hear about the guy from Rome who wanted to swim the English Channel but couldn't?

Geanie: No, what about him?
Gene: He could only swim in Italian.

❐

Rudolph: What goes into the water white and comes out blue?
Thelma: I'm blank.
Rudolph: A swimmer on a cold day.

T

Tailors

What did the dressmaker say?
Just sew-sew.

❐

Nit: What do you say to a tailor about his clothes?
Wit: I have no clue.
Nit: Suit yourself.

❐

Ferdinand: What would you call a tailor if you didn't know his name?
Gertrude: I have no clue.
Ferdinand: You'd call him "Mr. Sew-and-Sew."

❐

Why do dressmakers like the wide-open spaces?
They don't feel hemmed in.

Taxes

Sign in a service station:
We Collect Taxes—
Federal, State, and Local.
We also Sell Gasoline as a Sideline.

❐

Smith: I hate paying my tax bill.
Brown: You should pay up with a smile.
Smith: I've offered them a smile, but they insist on money.

Tea

Rob: Where do they keep the kettle on a ship?
Rachel: You tell me.
Rob: In the boiler room.

❐

Diner: Every time I have a cup of tea, I get a stabbing pain in my right eye. What shall I do?
Waiter: Take the spoon out of your cup.

❐

Kermit: What starts with T, ends with T, and is full of T?
Zackery: Search me.
Kermit: A teapot.

Teachers

What did the teacher say?
My work is classy.

❐

Who trains court jesters?
Fool teachers.

❐

Q: When does a teacher wear dark glasses?
A: When she has bright pupils.

❐

Lila: What do they call a textbook wired for sound?
Lillian: I have no clue.
Lila: A professor.

❐

I had one tough teacher: During the summer months he generally found work as the warden of a Turkish prison.

❐

Did you hear about the absent-minded professor? He returned from lunch and saw a sign on the door, "Back in 30 minutes," and sat down and waited for himself.

❐

I have the toughest teacher in the world. In most classes you bring an apple for the teacher. With this teacher you bring raw meat.

Teeth

What kind of teeth can you buy for a dollar?
Buck teeth.

❐

Jeff: What kind of toothpaste do you use?
Larry: I don't use any.
Jeff: How come?
Larry: My teeth aren't loose.

❐

Q: Why are false teeth like stars?
A: Because they come out at night.

Television

Nit: What is the other name for TV soap operas?
Wit: Who knows?
Nit: Dope operas.

❐

Q: Why is a television set like a railroad crossing?
A: Because it makes people stop, look, and listen.

❐

Television: Chewing gum for the eyes.

❐

What is the best part about owning tiny TV sets?
Tiny commercials.

❐

Jack: How many controls do you have on your TV set?
Mike: Six, most of the time—my father, my mother, and my four sisters.

❐

Geraldine: What is the strangest kind of commercial?
Gaspar: It's unknown to me.
Geraldine: An oddvertisement.

❐

Derek: What's the easiest way to get on TV?
Dorcus: I pass.
Derek: Sit on your set.

Tennis

Where is tennis mentioned in the Bible?
When Joseph served in Pharaoh's court.

❐

Gertrude: Why shouldn't you ever give your heart to a tennis player?
Gerard: I can't guess.
Gertrude: Because to him, love means nothing.

Ticks

Wilber: What part of the body do ticks like to bite?
Wanda: I'm blank.
Wilber: Ticks attack toes.

❐

Abner: What are the most loyal insects?
Agatha: I have no clue.
Abner: Ticks. Once they find friends, they stick to them.

❐

Art: What do you call little bugs that live on the moon?
Bart: That's a mystery.
Art: Luna-ticks.

Tigers

Ichabod: Who is safe when a man-eating tiger is loose?
Eutychus: I'm a blank.
Ichabod: Women and children.

❐

Where do you find tigers?
It depends on where you leave them.

❐

What steps should you take if a tiger charges you?
Long ones.

❐

First man: That's a beautiful stuffed tiger you've got there. Where did you get him?
Second man: In India when I was on a hunting expedition with my uncle.
First man: What is he stuffed with?
Second man: My uncle.

❐

Why do tigers have stripes?
Because they would look funny in polka dots.

❐

Claud: What did the man get when he crossed some cabbage with a tiger?
Chloe: I don't have the foggiest.
Claud: Man-eating coleslaw.

Time

Ichabod: If five dogs are chasing a cat down the street, what time is it?
Eutychus: I have no clue.
Ichabod: Five after one.

□

Doreen: Why did the runner bring his barber to the Olympics?
Duncan: I have no idea.
Doreen: He wanted to shave a few seconds off his time.

□

Jeff: What seems to be your trouble?
Joel: After I get up in the morning, I'm always dizzy for half an hour.
Jeff: Then why don't you get up half an hour later?

□

What is always coming but never arrives?
Tomorrow.

□

Gwendolyn: What time is it when the kids need a nap?
Godfrey: Tell me.
Gwendolyn: Whine o'clock.

□

How far is it from one end of the earth to the other?
A day's journey.

□

How do you make a slow employee fast?
Don't give him anything to eat for awhile.

□

Ambrose: What is the best way to make time go faster?
Stella: I have no idea.
Ambrose: Use the spur of the moment.

□

Why is a calendar so popular?
Because it has lots of dates.

❐

Q: If a father gives 15 cents to his son and a dime to his daughter, what time of day is it?
A: A quarter to two.

❐

Rudolph: What table is made of paper?
Thelma: Beats me.
Rudolph: A timetable.

❐

Ed: I hear the men are striking.
Jeff: What for?
Ed: Shorter hours.
Jeff: Good for them. I always did think sixty minutes was too long for an hour.

❐

Rudolph: What are the six main seasons?
Thelma: I have no clue.
Rudolph: Summer, fall, winter, spring, salt, and pepper.

❐

Nitrate (NI-trate): Cheapest price for calling long distance.

Train Engineers

Did you hear about the absentminded train conductor?
He lost track of things.

❐

What is the difference between a locomotive engineer and a schoolteacher?
One minds the train, and the other trains the mind.

❐

Q: How do locomotives hear?
A: Through their engineers (engine ears).

Travel

Clem: What should you do if you always get sick the night before a trip?
Slim: I don't know.
Clem: Start a day earlier.

❐

Greg: How was your trip to Helsinki?
Gean: Terrible! All our luggage vanished into Finn Air!

❐

Jon-Mark: If you were in line at a train ticket window and the man in front of you was going to Los Angeles and the lady in back of you was going to Florida, where would you be going?
Jonas: You've got me.
Jon-Mark: If you don't know, then what are you doing in line?

❐

Calvin: What do you think a Laplander is?
Cora: Beats me.
Calvin: Someone who can't keep his balance while riding a bus.

❐

Calvin: I would like to go on a boat trip, but I can't afford it.
Cora: I know. Beggars can't be cruisers.

❐

Rob: When are roads unpleasant?
Rachel: Search me.
Rob: When they are crossroads.

❐

What do you call a guy who likes to read road maps?
Miles.

Trees

Farmer: This is a dogwood tree.
Tourist: How can you tell?
Farmer: By its bark.

❐

What does a maple tree like to watch on TV?
Sap operas.

❐

Cyrus: What did the beaver say to the tree?
Cornelia: It's unknown to me.
Cyrus: It's been nice gnawing you.

❐

Abner: How can you recognize a dogwood tree?
Abigail: I have no clue.
Abner: By its bark.

❐

What do you get when you chop down a tuna tree?
Fish sticks.

❐

Abner: What is the difference between an oak tree and a tight shoe?
Agatha: I'm blank.
Abner: One makes acorns, and the other makes corns ache.

❐

Quentin: What tree is always very sad?
Obadiah: I give up.
Quentin: Weeping willow.

❐

What did the tree surgeon say?
I've some shady deals going.

❐

Debby: I just love to be in the country and hear the trees whisper.
Denise: That may be okay, but I hate to hear the grass mown.

❐

Luann: What does not break no matter how far it falls?
Lowell: Search me.
Luann: A leaf.

❐

Gertrude: What did the tree surgeon say to the diseased dogwood?
Gerard: I give up.
Gertrude: Your bark is worse than your blight.

❐

The only thing I know about my husband's family tree is that monkeys once lived in it.

❐

Q: There are seven maple trees and on the seven maple trees are seven branches and on the seven branches are seven acorns. How many acorns are there?
A: None. Acorns don't grow on maple trees.

Trouble

One kid in our class was always in trouble. I won't say his parents were called into school often, but his mom and dad had the lead in the school play.

❐

Edna: What is easy to get into but hard to get out of?
Eldon: I have no clue.
Edna: Trouble.

Trucks

Did you hear about the glue truck that overturned?
Police were asking motorists to stick to their own lanes.

Turkeys

Arnold: Why did the turkey cross the road?
Amy: My mind is blank.
Arnold: Because the chicken retired and moved to Florida.

❐

Gwendolyn: What do you call a formal dance for turkeys?
Godfrey: It's unknown to me.
Gwendolyn: A turkey trot.

❐

Q: Why do turkeys have small appetites?
A: Because they are always stuffed.

Turtles

Cyrus: What was the turtle doing on the freeway?
Cornelia: I have no clue.
Cyrus: About half a mile an hour.

❐

Turtle: A reptile who lives in a mobile home.

❐

Two turtles stopped to get a drink in a drugstore. When they ordered their sodas it started to rain. The big turtle said, "Go home and get an umbrella." The little turtle said, "Don't drink my soda while I'm gone."

Two years later the big turtle said, "I guess he isn't going to come back. I might as well drink it." A voice from outside said, "If you drink the soda, I won't go home."

❐

Cecil: What do turtles give each other?
Cyrus: Search me.
Cecil: People-neck sweaters.

❐

Loony turtle salesman: My business is very slow.

U

Umbrellas

She: Where did you get that umbrella?
He: It was a gift from sister.
She: You told me you hadn't any sisters.
He: I know. But that's what's engraved on the handle.

❐

Q: Why did the little boy take an umbrella to church?
A: Because he heard the preacher was going to preach up a storm.

Vacuums

Bill: Why is a vacuum cleaner like a gossip?
Jill: I have no idea.
Bill: Because it picks up lots of dirt.

Vegetables

Ichabod: Is the joker animal, vegetable, or mineral?
Eutychus: I can't guess.
Ichabod: Vegetable . . . he's a human bean.

❒

Geneva: What two garden vegetables fight crime?
Guthrie: I'm in the dark.
Geneva: Beetman and Radish.

❒

Peggy: How do you catch celery?
Paul: That's a mystery.
Peggy: You stalk it.

❒

Levi: Why did the man have to go to the hospital after a tomato fell on his head?
Lois: You tell me.
Levi: It was in a can.

❒

Cyrus: What is green, then purple, then green, then purple?
Cornelia: Who knows?
Cyrus: A pickle that works part-time as a grape.

❒

Bill: Why do pickles laugh when you touch them?
Jill: I can't guess.
Bill: They're pickle-ish.

❐

Geneva: What do you call a carrot that insults a farmer?
Guthrie: I give up.
Geneva: A fresh vegetable.

❐

Gloria: Did you hear about the head of cabbage, the hose, and the bottle of ketchup that were having a race?
Gretta: No, how did it go?
Gloria: The cabbage was ahead, the hose was still running, and the bottle of ketchup was trying to catch up.

❐

What has a heart in its head?
Lettuce.

❐

What will stay hot the longest in the refrigerator?
Red pepper.

❐

Luann: Why is it dangerous for farmers to plant peas during a war?
Lowell: I don't know.
Luann: The enemy might come along and shell them.

❐

Loony lima bean: I had a date with a green bean, but I think she only went out with me because of the money I spent on her.
Loony pork 'n' bean: I think she's stringing you along.

❐

Loony teacher: Do ears of corn get dandruff?
Loony student: Sure. Haven't you ever heard of corn flakes?

❐

What is orange, runs on batteries, and costs 6 million dollars?
The Bionic Carrot.

❐

Baby corn: Mommy, who brought me?
Mother corn: The stalk brought you!

❐

Q: If a carrot and a cabbage have a race, which will win?
A: The cabbage, because it's ahead.

❐

Q: Where can you see man-eating plants?
A: In a vegetarian restaurant!

❐

Abner: What's red and goes up and down?
Agatha: I'm in the dark.
Abner: A tomato in an elevator.

❐

You peel the outside, boil the inside, nibble on the outside, and throw
the inside into the garbage. What is it?
Corn on the cob.

❐

Ambrose: What is green and sings?
Stella: I pass.
Ambrose: Elvis Parsley.

❐

Ambrose: What is green, noisy, and extremely dangerous?
Stella: How should I know?
Ambrose: A stampeding herd of pickles.

❐

Did you ever see a salad bowl?

❐

Quentin: What vegetable hurts when you step on it?
Obadiah: I don't have the foggiest.
Quentin: Corn.

Ventriloquists

Once upon a time there was a loony ventriloquist who was so bad, you could see his lips move even when he wasn't saying anything.

❐

Ventriloquist: A person who talks to himself for a living.

W

Walls

What do you call a guy who's been hung up on the wall by his belt?
Art.

❐

What do you call a guy whom everyone hangs pictures on?
Wally.

❐

What do you call a girl who stands next to walls?
Lena.

❐

What invention allows people to walk through walls?
Doors.

Watches

Did your watch stop when it fell on the floor?
Sure. Did you think it would go right on through?

❐

Laurel: What is always behind time?
LaVonne: I give up.
Laurel: The back of a watch.

❐

I'm really unlucky. My parents bought me a wristwatch that's water-proof, shockproof, and rustproof. I had it three days and it caught fire.

❐

What is the difference between a jeweler and a jailer?
One sells watches while the other watches cells.

❐

Q: Why is a watch like a river?
A: Because it doesn't run long without winding.

Water

What do you call a guy who's been dropped into the middle of the ocean?
Bob.

❏

Claud: What kind of water can't be frozen?
Chloe: I pass.
Claud: Boiling water.

❏

Q: How did Hiawatha?
A: With thoap and water.

❏

What should you do if you find yourself with water on the knee, water on the elbow, and water on the brain?
Turn off the shower.

❏

Clem: What can you add to a bucket of water that makes it weigh less?
Slim: I'm in the dark.
Clem: Holes.

❏

Luann: What is the surest way to keep water from coming into your house?
Lowell: You tell me.
Luann: Don't pay the water bill.

❏

What is full of holes but holds water?
A sponge.

❏

Lydia: How can you tell the difference between the land and the ocean?
Larry: You tell me.
Lydia: The land is dirty and the ocean is tide-y.

❏

Q: Why is a river rich?
A: Because it always has two banks.

❏

Willard: If you wanted to take a bath without water, what would you do?
Wallace: I can't guess.
Willard: Take a sunbath.

❏

What happens when the human body is completely submerged in water?
The telephone rings.

❏

Geraldine: What do you get when you cross a stream with a brook?
Gaspar: My mind is blank.
Geraldine: Wet feet.

❏

Cornelius: What lies at the bottom of the sea and wriggles?
Henrietta: I have no clue.
Cornelius: A nervous wreck.

❏

Flood: A river that's too big for its bridges.

❏

Surfing: A tide ride.

❏

Ryan: What could you call the small rivers that flow into the Nile?
Mark: My mind's a blank.
Ryan: Juveniles.

❏

What do you call a guy who's been thrown across the surface of a pond? Skip.

❒

Q: How can you carry water in a sieve?
A: Make it into a block of ice first.

❒

Sir Cecil: After my ship went down, I survived a week in the open sea on just a can of sardines.
Lady Alice: Goodness, however did you keep from falling off?

Weather

Beastly weather: Raining cats and dogs.

❒

What is worse than raining cats and dogs?
Hailing taxis and buses.

❒

Luann: What is the best weather for gathering hay?
Lowell: I'm in the dark.
Luann: When it rains pitchforks.

❒

Christy: Is there any difference between lightning and electricity?
Quentin: Yes. You don't have to pay for lightning.

❒

Clem: What goes over hill and vale, makes a noise but never leaves a trail?
Slim: I have no idea.
Clem: The wind.

❒

Lola: When rain falls, does it ever get up again?
Lionel: You've got me guessing.
Lola: Oh, yes—in dew time.

❒

What does a tire do when it rains?
It gets wet.

❐

Q: Why does lightning shock people?
A: Because it doesn't know how to conduct itself.

❐

Lila: What falls often but never gets hurt?
Lillian: I have no idea.
Lila: Rain.

❐

Q: Why can't it rain for two days continually?
A: Because there is always a night in between.

❐

Mrs. Lilley: Noel, go outside and water the garden.
Noel: But Mom, it's raining.
Mrs. Lilley: So put your raincoat on.

❐

Coincide: What you should do when it rains.

❐

Ambrose: What's white and goes up?
Stella: Who knows?
Ambrose: A dumb snowflake.

❐

Cecil: What is an eavesdropper?
Cyrus: I have no clue.
Cecil: An icicle.

❐

Kermit: What's the right kind of lumber for castles in the air?
Zackery: My mind's a blank.
Kermit: Sunbeams.

Weathermen

Did you hear about the weatherman who went back to college?
He got several degrees.

❐

Doreen: Why didn't the weatherman ever get tired?
Duncan: I give up.
Doreen: He always got a second wind.

❐

Barnaby: Why was the weatherman arrested?
Barbie: That's a mystery.
Barnaby: For shooting the breeze.

❐

Did you hear about the weatherman who won the race?
He said it was a breeze.

Whales

Jeff: What do you say to a crying whale?
Joel: You've got me.
Jeff: Quit your blubbering.

Windows

Barnaby: Why didn't the kitchen window like the living room window?
Barbie: My mind is blank.
Barnaby: Because it was such a big pane.

❐

Dora: In the summer I get up as soon as the first ray of sun comes in my window.
Flora: Isn't that a bit early?
Dora: No, my window faces west.

❐

Kermit: What Jack paints people's windows?
Zackery: I have no clue.
Kermit: Jack Frost.

❏

Cecil: What pain do we make light of?
Cyrus: You tell me.
Cecil: Windowpane.

❏

Kermit: What gadget do we use to see through walls?
Zackery: It's unknown to me.
Kermit: A window.

❏

Leah: What do they call the device that keeps flies in the house?
Lawrence: I don't have the foggiest.
Leah: A window screen.

❏

Teacher: John, do you know anything about this broken window?
John: Well, sort of . . .
Teacher: What happened?
John: I was cleaning my slingshot, and it went off accidentally.

Wives

Nicky: Look at that couple over there arguing. Boy, he sure is henpecked.
Vicky: How can you tell? They're not speaking. They're using sign language.
Nicky: Yes, but just look. He can't get a finger in edgewise!

❏

Carter: My wife writes me that she is all unstrung. What shall I do?
Clara: You tell me.
Carter: Maybe I should send her a wire.

❏

Loony wife: Wake up! Wake up! There's a burglar in the kitchen, and he's eating the leftover stew we had for supper.

Loony husband: Go back to sleep and don't worry, dear. I'll bury him in the morning.

❐

My wife allows no eating in the living room. She's sort of a one-woman food and rug administrator.

❐

Man: I saved my wife a lot of standing in line this Christmas. I didn't give her a present.

Friend: How's that?

Man: I gave her an exchange certificate. Who needs a middleman?

❐

Loony boy: They call a man's wife his better half, don't they?

Loony father: Yes, they do.

Loony boy: Then I guess if a man marries twice, there's nothing left of him.

❐

Joe: Did you know that Kendall gave his wife a three-hundred-piece set of dishes for Christmas?

Moe: That was very nice of him.

Joe: Well, it was only supposed to be twenty-four pieces, but he tripped coming home from the store.

❐

Husband: I gave you a mink coat for Christmas and you still weren't satisfied.

Wife: You know I'd rather have a Cadillac than a mink.

Husband: Sure, but where can I get an imitation Cadillac?

❐

Wife: My husband thinks he's a TV antenna.

Doctor: I think I can cure him.

Wife: I don't want him cured, just adjusted. I can't get channel 47.

❐

Husband: My wife served a beautiful meal last night. Meat loaf in one corner of the plate, mashed potatoes in another corner of the plate, and brussel sprouts in another corner. She has to put them all in separate corners so we can tell them apart.

Wood

Q: When is a piece of wood like a queen?
A: When it is made into a ruler.

❏

Q: When is a rope like a piece of wood?
A: When it has knots.

❏

Pipe cleaner: A toothpick with long underwear.

❏

Q: How did the wood shaving fly from the board?
A: It took off on a plane.

❏

She was born on her parents' wooden anniversary so they called her "Peg."

Worms

Ambrose: What happened to the two silk worms that had a race?
Agatha: Beats me.
Ambrose: They ended up in a tie.

❏

Geneva: What does a worm do in a cornfield?
Guthrie: I don't have a clue.
Geneva: It goes in one ear and out the other.

❏

Ambrose: What is worse than finding a worm in an apple?
Stella: Beats me.
Ambrose: Finding half a worm.

❏

Q: What do you get when you cross a worm and a fur coat?
A: A caterpillar.

Z

Zebras

Lisa: What is black and white and yellow?
Lucile: My mind is blank.
Lisa: A bus full of zebras.

❐

What is black and white and hides in caves?
A zebra who owes money.

❐

A zebra with wide stripes married a zebra with narrow stripes. Their first son had no stripes. What did they call him?
Leroy.

❐

Quentin: What is black and white and has sixteen wheels?
Obadiah: I don't know.
Quentin: A zebra on roller skates.

Zoos

What did the zookeeper say?
It's beastly!

❐

Q: What has an elephant's trunk, a giraffe's neck, a bird's beak, and a lion's head?
A: A zoo.

❐

Zoo: A place where animals look at silly people.